To Kendall and Brady

FINANCIAL DECISIONS IN LIFE

**First edition. March 13, 2025.**



ISBN: 979-8230154112

Written by Donald Pickinpaugh.

# Acknowledgments

I would like to thank my fantastic wife for her patience and for encouraging me to write this book. I would also like to thank Bette James, Anne Heskett, and Jan Pickinpaugh for editing. In addition, I would like to thank Calvin Balsam, Kurt Schoen, Courtney Yartz, and Bob Candido for their suggestions. The "Golden Egg" cover has been designed using assets from Freepik.com.

# Introduction

I always had to have a flight plan when flying missions in the Air Force. My flight plan would provide me with many options along my route if I encountered any unexpected events. Even though I was flying alone in the cockpit, I had many resources to call upon for assistance. This book follows those same principles and provides financial options to handle unexpected events along your financial flight plan.

Financial decisions in life can be overwhelming. The rules and regulations are changed daily by the government entities in charge.

We all have to start somewhere with a budget and work from there. For over a decade, I was living paycheck to paycheck. It took me years to understand the importance of a budget and to commit to living within my means. The Bible states that the borrower is the servant to the lender. I can verify this is true. There is no freedom in living life in the debt bubble.

Our journey through life is a learning process. Along that path, we will come face to face with decisions that will impact our daily finances. At various points in my lifetime, I have made many mistakes, only later to realize I should have spent more time and effort researching before making a financial decision. Do not feel bad if you make a mistake; own it and move on. Refrain from dwelling on past events, which will not help your current situation. There will be many times you will wish you had made a different financial choice. We always remember the financial decisions that got away and somehow forget the boring investments that are on a path to create wealth for us. Keep your eyes on the prize before you.

We can leave our financial decisions to someone else, but ultimately, we are the responsible parties.

This book will give you an overview and some thoughts to consider when making financial decisions. I cover most of the financial topics I believe you may encounter throughout your lifetime. You will encounter some financial topics not covered in this book, but the decision-making process is all the same. Discuss each financial topic with your spouse before coming to an agreement. My spouse prides herself in asking me many tough questions, thus preventing me from making financial mistakes in our marriage. She is my financial safety net and the reason I was able to retire.

Practically all financial rules and regulations are on government websites since the Fed is the governing body. Try to stick to these websites, as non-government entities can provide you with misinformation. The financial field is highly complex and can change in the blink of an eye. Finding the information you seek will take only a few minutes, and you will be on your way to financial freedom. Congratulations on taking the first step towards that freedom.

# Topics

# Chapter 1

## Tranquility at Home

First and foremost, the purpose of the most crucial financial decisions will be tranquility at home. What do I mean by that? You will inevitably have financial disagreements between you and your spouse. However, how you both work out those disagreements will be critical in handling financial decisions throughout your lifetime. If you are single, you have to answer only to yourself, but realize that you should always get a second opinion regarding your finances.

You are in the wrong position if either spouse is too stubborn and is locked into a decision. Nearly 40% of divorces list finances as one of the significant causes of separation. So, it is in your best interest to work through any disagreements. Divorce can reduce your assets faster than making a mistake on any topic I will discuss. You need to make the financial decisions together, but sometimes you will have differences. That is understandable. How you work through those differences will bring tranquility to your home.

First, you must listen to your spouse if he or she disagrees with your assessment on a topic and the direction you want to proceed. I once read a wise statement from someone who said no human being can learn while talking. That statement says a lot. Sometimes, it's just best to shut up and listen to your spouse's opinions and concerns. If you are listening, then you can do no harm.

Second, you will need to make some compromises to get to an agreeable solution. My wife and I even go as far as to shake hands on our compromises.

Third, follow up to ensure your decisions are on track and you are still satisfied with the outcome.

What if one spouse wants the other to make all the financial decisions? If this is the case, I still recommend you explain your plan and ask your spouse if there are any suggestions or opinions. Your spouse will then at least be part of the conversation and feel their opinion is valued. This process will let the spouse know about financial decisions and the costs associated with those decisions. For example, imagine a husband who recently died and the spouse did not know where their important papers were. The wife knew they had life insurance for her husband but could not find the policy. Unfortunately, the wife did not even have the combination to the safe, which contained all their estate documents. Life insurance papers were never located, even after hiring a locksmith to open the safe. To avoid this situation, make sure your spouse knows all the information on financial decisions and where your necessary documents are located. I will cover this information thoroughly in the topic "In Case I Die Letter."

Another example of tranquility at home is when a friend obtained a historically low 3% mortgage rate for their house. After retirement, my friend and his spouse discussed whether to pay off their home with some of their assets from their retirement account. The low 3% fixed rate was hard to beat on paper, but his wife felt uncomfortable retiring with a large house debt hanging over their heads. At first, my friend struggled with the thought of pulling a large sum of money from their investments to pay off their house. In the end, they did pay off their entire mortgage. This compromise is a perfect example of agreeing to a solution both spouses can live with and maintain tranquility at home.

Overall, it is a great feeling for couples to be comfortable with their financial decisions. If you or your spouse are having trouble sleeping at night with the decisions you have made, then you are not at peace.

Continue discussions with your spouse until you have a decision you both can live with and sleep soundly. Remember, neither you nor your spouse knows how the future will turn out. No one can predict the best financial decision until the future has come to pass. Also, DO NOT look back and boast if you guessed the right financial decision and your spouse did not. Do not let your pride get the best of you. Make a decision together, and then don't look back.

# Chapter 2

## Knowing Your Budget

P*urpose* - Creating wealth starts with budgeting. You need to know how much money is coming in and how much money is going out.

*Highlights* - Growing up, I borrowed money for whatever I wanted and didn't think about how to pay the loan. That thought I put off until another day. I also prided myself on paying the minimum balance on my credit card each month, not knowing the interest rate I was being charged. I can blame only myself and tell you this is no way to live. I constantly wondered if my checks would clear the bank and often ran out of money three days before payday. When I got married, my wife immediately changed my way of thinking; thank goodness she did.

What is wealth? Everyone will have a different answer to that question. I always assumed it was a point where you have enough money to retire comfortably and not worry about your bills daily. Whatever your definition of wealth is, you will have to start somewhere, which usually involves saving and investing. First, you will need to know your budget.

When I ask people about their yearly budget, I usually get a blank stare or a long pause on the phone. Very few people actually know how much money they spend a year. Calculating a yearly budget is simple, but many people will need help to sit down and run the numbers. This behavior is understandable, as I didn't know my annual budget for many years either. People can usually tell you right off the bat how much money they make per year, but how much they spend is sometimes elusive.

I find it challenging to do a monthly budget, since some bills come due in different months of the year. Your vacation bill may come due in the summer, whereas yearly car insurance payments may happen in other months. The easiest way to calculate a budget is on an annual basis.

Knowing your "working years" budget to determine how much money you have available to invest is critical. Once you know your budget, you can establish a plan, set goals, and then reevaluate your strategy to see if you are meeting your objectives.

There are a few calculations required to figure out your yearly budget. My formula and yours may be slightly different. Mine is pretty simple: Income - taxes - tithing - budget = amount left over for investments. The budget part of this formula is the most challenging piece of the puzzle to calculate. Once you know how much you need for your budget, you will know what is left over for investments.

The income piece of the formula is the most straightforward since you can look at your end-of-year paycheck or your W2 for your annual salary.

Most of your taxes will come from your paychecks and are easy to find. Again, your year-end paycheck or W-2 will list all the taxes you paid throughout the year. Generally, six taxes can affect your take-home pay: Federal Taxes, State Taxes, Local Taxes, Social Security Taxes, Medicare Taxes, and additional Medicare Taxes for some higher-income earners. Some people may have a couple of rare add-on taxes. Also, depending on where you live, your state may have fewer or more taxes than I listed above.

If you tithe, you will need to calculate how much you tithe throughout the year. This step is also relatively easy to calculate from your yearly salary or church statement.

Next is the most challenging part: your budget. You must sit down with your spouse and calculate all your monthly bills over the entire year. As mentioned earlier, some bills may be due in different months, so multiplying one month by 12 may not accurately capture your yearly expenses. A computer finance program or a checkbook can simplify this task rather than reviewing your bank records. My spouse and I still use a checkbook.

Once you figure out how much you spend each year, you can then get an idea if you have any money left over for investments. If no money is left over after your expenses, then your salary is your budget. If this is the case, you will need to concentrate on controlling your expenses, which I will cover in the next chapter.

If you have money left over after calculating your budget, you are on the right path. For example, if you make $72,000 per year and owe $14,400 in taxes and $7,200 in tithing, you are left with a yearly budget of $38,400. In this scenario, let's say you have $12,000 left to invest. Of that $12,000 per year investment, you might have $6,000 per year going to an employer 401K plan and then invest the other $6,000 into an Individual Retirement Account (IRA). Investing $12,000 annually is 16.6% of your salary. Great job.

In the above example, you had an extra 16% of your salary you could use for investments. With this number in mind, you can then break down each paycheck to set your goals. Realize that since some yearly bills will come due at different times, not every paycheck will meet that percentage for investments. First, you must determine your investment goals and what you are comfortable with. Can you invest 10% of your salary towards investments? Maybe 20%? Remember, the higher your investment goals, the more you must control your budget. Try to keep things in balance as you and your spouse must set realistic investment goals. Leave a little buffer each paycheck, since each month can have smaller, unexpected bills you might not have planned for. If you have any buffer money left over before the next paycheck, you can invest that, too. We will review Emergency Savings in a few chapters to protect you from larger unforeseen bills.

As you consider your investment plan, you might ask if it is unrealistic to be able to have $1,000,000 in investments before retirement. Absolutely not. After activating your plan, you must analyze it regularly to see if you are meeting the investment goals you both agreed upon. I like to do this on my end-of-year financial checklist and discuss it with my spouse to see if she has any changes or if we should continue our current course of action.

After calculating your budget to see if any money is available for investments, you and your spouse must determine where you want that investment to go. We will discuss some investment vehicles later, including 401Ks, IRAs, and 529s.

My father-in-law always tells me, "You must have a plan." This idea probably evolved from his father dying of a heart attack in his arms at age 15. As a boy, he had to grow up quickly, and soon after, he joined the Army and started sending his paychecks home so his mom could survive. Wanting to go to college and having no money, he spent significant amounts of time in the library applying for over 70 scholarships to be able to go to college for free. So, having a plan and setting some goals is vital, and don't be afraid to go after a dream.

*Thoughts* - The biggest threat to your budget is impulse spending. If this is a problem, you will need to set some boundaries. My wife and I have a rule that if we want to buy any non-essential item over $50, we must ask permission from the other spouse. This requirement holds us accountable to each other and to our budget.

Another idea that may help you stay on budget is calculating how much money you have available to spend daily. You can divide your estimated monthly budget by 30, giving you a daily spending amount. If your paychecks are every two weeks, divide by 14 instead of 30. If I spend over my daily amount on a particular day, I try to spend less the next day. This method does not always work, but it helps me stay on track with my budget.

One rule of thumb in the industry is the 50/30/20 budget recommendation. These percentages recommend you use 50% of your budget for items you need, 30% for things you want, and 20% for savings. If you meet this recommendation, you are on the pathway to creating wealth.

If only one spouse is earning an income, it is beneficial for the non-salary spouse to have a monthly budget to purchase household items. This budget must be agreed upon so the non-salary spouse does not have to ask permission to buy items required to meet the household's needs. Remember, having a spouse stay home with kids is an investment in the future of those children, and that investment needs to be funded. Taking care of children and the household is a full-time, non-paying job. I classify this job as the toughest job out there.

To add to that thought, if only one spouse has a salary, I suggest the working spouse fund some of that spouse's retirement accounts. This funding will ensure the non-salaried spouse is part of the budgetary and investment process and feels included in the family finances. Some of those investments can consist of IRAs, brokerage accounts, and 529 accounts, where the person owns those accounts. For example, suppose the working spouse has their 401k contributions automatically deducted from paychecks. If you have any extra money after your budget, you can invest that towards an Individual Retirement Account

(IRA) for your spouse who does not have a salary. This effort will pay dividends throughout your marriage.

If both spouses have salary-paying jobs, you still need to work together on budgeting and where to direct any extra money toward investments. Avoid getting into the "I make more, but you spend more" argument. You both are a team and need to be on the same page. Compromise can save you a lot of headaches.

Finally, if you use a credit card to purchase everything, deduct the amount directly from your running budget so you can have an accurate balance. I personally deduct the amount straight out of my checkbook at the time of purchase. Then, when I get my credit card statement, I just write a check for the balance since it has already been deducted from my budget. Today, many people use debit or credit cards instead of checks to handle all their finances. That is okay as long as you have a system to know your balance at any given time. Refrain from blowing through your budget, as a credit card can make that easy to do. If you do not have the money for a purchase, wait until you do.

# Chapter 3

## Controlling Your Expenses

P*urpose* - Controlling your expenses can save you money in both the short and the long term.

*Highlights* - If your budget is out of control or you spend more than you make, you are in trouble and need to fix this fast. I was listening to a financial radio show one day when a caller phoned in and said he had a financial problem. He was spending $3.5 million yearly while making only $3 million. You would think a person making $3 million a year would be in great shape, but even high-income earners can let their spending get out of control.

Whereas I like to view my budget on a yearly basis, I like to review my expenses on a monthly basis. If you need more money to meet your budget, controlling your expenses is much easier than trying to increase wages. Every year, mainly during the winter months, when we are stuck inside, my wife and I will look at all our monthly expenses and see what we can trim. We treat this process as a game more than anything. We set a goal on how much we want to save and then set out calling the billing companies.

I generally start with the phone companies. You can call them and ask them if they have any discounts or promotional sales. Generally, all the major phone companies will offer a corporate or military discount. Also, if you have been a customer with them for some time, they can give you a lower fee. I signed up for direct pay and saved $20 monthly with Verizon. Second, if you have a landline that you still pay for but don't use, you may consider dropping it to save additional money. Before eliminating that bill, ensure your landline is not connected to your security system. Still, with today's new technology, you can connect a wireless system to your security and eliminate your landline bill altogether.

Cable TV bills have gone through the roof. You may be able to use Sling or Hulu to save money. If that is not an option, ask the cable company to see what discounts are available and if they have any bundling options. Many times, these companies will try their best to get you some discounts so they do not lose you entirely as a customer. I gave up on cable TV 26 years ago and was surprised I didn't miss it. I currently have 56 free channels with a simple antenna installed. Taking the scissors to my cable bill has saved me tens of thousands of dollars over the years.

If you are an empty nester, you may not need that high-speed internet if the kids are out of the house. Unless you are into video games, you can probably live with less internet speed and thus save some money.

My security company offered me a $5 monthly savings if I agreed to a 3-year contract with them. I agreed. Sure, it's not a lot of money, but it is $180 over three years.

Are you bundling your car, house, and umbrella insurance? Generally, you can save money by bundling everything with the same insurance company. Also, if you have been with a company for quite some time, it may be beneficial to start comparing rates to other insurance agencies. Sometimes, we don't realize how much our insurance rates go up each year and are shocked to find out that the same amount of insurance coverage is cheaper elsewhere. I saved $1,700 yearly using an insurance broker and got more coverage.

Gym memberships may also have corporate or military rates. Check with other gyms to see if you can get a better rate, and then see if your gym will match a competitor's price.

Electric and gas bills are more challenging to reduce. A smart thermostat can help control your home's heating and air conditioning bills. I installed another layer of insulation in my attic and, at the same time, installed two hybrid electric water heaters, saving me nearly $1,200 per year in electricity bills. I also received a government rebate on the insulation and the water heaters.

*Thoughts* - I could cover many more expenses, but I wanted you to get an idea of some everyday expenses most of us have. Remember, by investing the savings, you also have the potential to increase those savings with investment returns over the years.

After trying to trim all the expenses you can think of, you may want to see if you can auto-pay any bills with a credit card. If the billing company charges you extra for using a credit card, then I would pass on that option. If you have a credit card that can pay you 2% back into an investment account, you can save a lot of money over time. I did precisely this for several decades, using the money to fund a 529 account to help pay for college for a niece. Remember to pay off your monthly credit card bill and get a credit card with no annual fees. If you do not pay off your credit card bill each month, you are defeating the purpose of trying to cut expenses while at the same time borrowing money from the credit card company with a very high interest rate. Let the credit card company pay you.

# Chapter 4

Employer Healthcare, Medishare, HSA's, FSA's, and HRA's

P*urpose* - Employer-sponsored health insurance is called a "group plan," and the employer will share the cost of this plan with employees.

*Highlights* - Many employers will offset the cost of their health plans up to a certain percentage. Some insurance companies may list the cost splits in the plan title, like a 90/10 split. This cost split means that if you had services rendered that are subject to coinsurance, your insurance company would pay 90% of the bill, and you pay 10%. Another popular plan is the 80/20 split. Having the company share in the costs makes these healthcare plans more affordable and benefits employees and their families. Generally, the lower your deductible and co-pay, the higher your monthly premiums will be. Usually, employer-sponsored healthcare plans come in two formats: HMOs and PPOs.

Health Maintenance Organizations (HMOs) plans offer health insurance that covers healthcare costs for people who go to doctors within the HMO network. HMO plans typically have lower associated expenses and out-of-pocket costs. Premiums are usually lower for in-network visits, and you are responsible only for the co-pay. Typically, there are no deductibles for HMOs. However, HMOs are more restrictive than Preferred Provider Organization (PPO) plans. With an HMO plan, you can access out-of-network doctors only if you get a referral. You will likely have to select a Primary Care Physician (PCP) to coordinate all your medical appointments. If you need specialized care, you will need a referral from your PCP. Also, your services under an HMO plan may be limited to only medically necessary procedures.

The Preferred Provider Organization (PPO) is the most common employer-sponsored insurance plan. Typically, PPOs have higher monthly premiums and out-of-pocket costs than HMO plans. You will have to meet the plan's deductible before insurance will pay, and then you may still be responsible for a certain percentage of the costs after the deductible is met. With PPO plans, you do not need to select a PCP, and you do not have to get a referral to see a doctor out of network, though the costs will generally be lower if you see an in-network provider. With a PPO plan, you get more flexibility as you can see what doctor you want and whenever you want, whereas this may not be an option under most HMO plans. Under a PPO plan, you will have to take on more responsibility for managing and coordinating your medical care since you may not have a PCP as you would under an HMO plan.

You may also see an employer offer a high deductible plan. Both HMOs and PPOs can have high deductible plans. A high deductible plan is considered an insurance plan with a deductible of at least $1,650 for an individual or $3,300 for a family in 2025. The deductible is the amount you pay out of pocket for medical expenses before your insurance pays anything. A high-deductible health plan can make sense if you are healthy or single and rarely get sick or injured. This type of plan may be a good choice if you have no existing medical conditions and can afford to pay the high deductible out of pocket if an unexpected medical expense arises. A high-deductible plan will have lower monthly premiums.

Medishare is a healthcare-sharing program where all members will share other members' medical bills. Medishare is not health insurance. With traditional health insurance, you pay for only your family's medical bills. Medishare can be a cheaper option than traditional healthcare insurance since it is a nonprofit organization. Medishare Complete has four tier levels of coverage, all based on your annual deductible. The higher the deductible, the lower the monthly share amount. Since this monthly share amount is not a premium like standard healthcare, you cannot use health savings accounts to pay for these share amounts. Health savings accounts will pay for any out-of-pocket costs with Medishare. For 2025, a $12,000 annual deductible will have a monthly share cost of $436 for a family of two. Medishare Complete also has three other annual deductible tiers of $9,000, $6,000, and $3,000. With a $3,000 yearly deductible, the share amount is the highest at $898 monthly. Your pricing may vary by state, marital status, and age.

As you can see, the lower the annual deductible, the higher the monthly share amount you will have to pay. Medishare may be a good choice if you have no pre-existing conditions and are in relatively good health.

Enrolling in a high-deductible plan may make you eligible to participate in a Health Savings Account or HSA. An HSA is a health savings account in which you can set aside money on a pre-tax basis to pay for any qualified medical, dental, or vision expenses you may have. The funds will also grow tax-free over time and can be used for qualified medical expenses tax-free. The maximum amount of money you can put into an HSA in 2025 is $4,300 for an individual and $8,550 for a family. In 2025, if you are older than age 55, you can contribute an extra $1,000 per person.

You can also use your HSA to pay co-payments, deductibles, and coinsurance. The balance in your HSA account will roll over each year and be combined with the following year's contributions. HSAs do not expire; you can use them until your account is empty. Former military personnel who qualify for Tricare cannot contribute to an HSA if they use Tricare as their primary or secondary insurance.

Another medical savings plan is called a Flex Spending Account (FSA). An agreement through your employer will let you pay for the same medical expenses that an HSA will pay for with tax-free dollars. You do not have to sign up for a medical plan to enroll in an FSA. You decide how much to put in an FSA, up to a limit set by your employer. However, an FSA has more limitations. The IRS use-or-lose rule states that FSA funds must be spent by the participant within the FSA's plan year. Unused funds at the plan year's end are forfeited and revert back to the plan.

Some employers may also offer a Health Reimbursement Arrangement (HRA). These are typically employer-funded healthcare savings plans from which employees are reimbursed for qualified medical expenses up to a fixed dollar amount per year. Any unused funds may be rolled over and used in subsequent years.

*Thoughts* - I have participated in both HMOs and PPOs. If you have a great Primary Care Physician you like, then the HMO is generally cheaper. As you get older, have kids, and expect more trips to the hospital, the PPO plan may offer more freedom and choices.

If you choose a high deductible plan, I recommend contributing as much as you can afford to the HSA, as any unused monies will roll over each year. Even if you have built up a large cash balance in your HSA upon retirement, you can use those funds to pay for Medicare Part B and D premiums and any out-of-pocket medical costs. In addition, you can also use any HSA money to pay long-term care premiums.

If your employer offers only an FSA plan, you must discuss with your spouse how much you want to contribute each year since any unused monies will revert to the plan.

According to Fidelity Investments, in 2022, a retired couple can expect to spend $315,000 for medical expenses for the remainder of their lives. This future expense is where an HSA can help offset those costs tax-free. Medical expenses post-age 65 only seem to go up each year.

The biggest shock for me in retirement was our medical expenses. With each passing year, individuals have to bear the brunt of higher healthcare costs. When you turn 65, Medicare premiums and other medical bills become more expensive each year.

# Chapter 5

Life and Accidental Death & Dismemberment Insurance

P*urpose* - Life insurance can protect you and your family from expenses arising after an unexpected death and provide replacement income.

*Highlights* - You may want to get life insurance once you have a family or if you care for dependents. Life insurance can provide tax-free income or replacement income.

Life insurance is generally divided into two main types: term life insurance and permanent life insurance. Permanent life insurance also has various options.

Term life insurance can provide money to cover school debt, mortgages, or even credit card debt so as not to burden the family with the loss of an income earner. You can lock in term life insurance for any number of years that fits your budget. For example, you can sign up to pay premiums for 5, 10, 15, and even 20-year periods where the rates will not increase. Some employers may offer group term life insurance where the rates only increase at 5-year intervals. However, term life has no cash value option, because it is cheaper than permanent life insurance.

Three popular permanent life insurance policies are whole life, universal life, and variable life Insurance.

Whole life insurance provides coverage for your lifetime. It is the most common type of permanent life insurance since your premiums will remain the same for your lifetime. Your policy will build cash value over time. Generally, the cash value will earn a fixed income rate set by the insurer. If you have accumulated enough in your cash value plan, you can borrow from the account or even use the money to pay your insurance premiums. If you want lifelong insurance coverage, then a whole life policy may be what you are looking for, although it is generally considered the most expensive of the three permanent life insurance policies.

Universal life insurance can offer you a flexible insurance policy. You may want the flexibility to adjust your premiums or death benefits up or down depending on changes in your lifetime. Adjusting your premiums can also change the cash value of the policy. With this flexibility, universal life may be more or less expensive than whole life, depending on what flexible options you choose to implement.

A variable life insurance policy will also have a guaranteed death benefit, but the cash value is not guaranteed. It is a type of permanent life insurance like whole and universal life, where you can invest your cash value savings into various other investment options like mutual funds. You have the potential to earn more money than in a fixed-rate policy, but you also can lose money. A variable life policy can carry more risk than whole and universal policies.

Accidental Death and Dismemberment (AD&D) Insurance is the cheapest of the life insurance policies. AD&D may be offered as a standalone policy through your employer or as a rider option with a life insurance policy. Employers may offer AD&D as a benefit to their employees at no cost. The reason AD&D is so cheap is because it will pay only if you die by accident or have a dismemberment of a body part. The policy usually pays a percentage of the total value insured if you lose a body part. There are some exclusions for AD&D. Those exclusions may include, but are not limited to, suicide or attempted suicide, intentional injuries, wartime injuries or death, and injury or death while committing a felony.

*Thoughts* - To determine how much life insurance you may need, determine how much income you want to replace. If you have a taxable income of $100,000 and pay $30,000 in Federal, State, Local, Medicare, and Social Security taxes, this will leave you with $70,000 per year after taxes. So, you will want to replace this $70,000 with tax-free life insurance to get equal compensation. I would use a conservative 5% return on your investment, requiring a $1.4 million life insurance policy to give you a tax-free income of $70,000 annually.

Whether you have a family or not, AD&D insurance is a great value considering the cost. Take advantage of this program if your employer offers it for free or at a reduced price. If the employer does not provide AD&D, purchase it through a private insurance company.

If you have a family or are single and have dependents that rely on your income, then purchase either term or permanent life insurance. If your employer offers a group policy, sign up for this option, where you can have your premiums taken right out of your paycheck so you will not miss the deduction. There will always be a debate on whether term or permanent life insurance is better. You will want to have this debate with your spouse or family members. If money is tight, you may have to go with term insurance. If, later in life, you are in a better financial position, then you may want to switch over to a permanent Life insurance option. Either type of insurance will protect you and your family.

# Chapter 6

## Disability Insurance, Workers Compensation, SSDI, and SSI

P*urpose* - Disability insurance can protect you and your family from an injury or sickness and provide you with continued income.

*Highlights* - You can purchase disability insurance privately or through your employer. You may also qualify for disability through the government Social Security program, which has two types of disability insurance: SSDI and SSI.

A middle-aged worker has a 400% greater chance of being disabled before dying, yet we always seem to get life insurance before disability insurance. Before purchasing disability insurance, you must determine what type and length of insurance you need. Some states may require that all employers offer disability insurance to their employees.

Short-term disability may cover you for up to six months and replace up to 70% of your income. Short-term disability policies also will have a shorter waiting period for you to qualify for benefits. This waiting period is generally called an elimination period and may be as short as seven days.

Long-term disability may provide a benefit from 1 to 20 years or until you reach retirement age. Whatever disability plan you choose, the timeframe the policy pays out is called the benefit period. Long-term disability generally has a longer elimination period than a short-term policy. The elimination period for a long-term policy may extend up to a year before benefits actually start.

Workers' Compensation is insurance that can provide cash benefits and medical care for workers who are injured or become ill directly due to their job. Employers pay for this insurance. The employer's insurance provider pays weekly cash benefits and medical care. A worker might lose their worker's compensation claim if their injury results from their intoxication from drugs or alcohol or from the intent to injure themselves or someone else. Once you return to work, your worker's compensation will end unless your injuries prevent you from making what you previously earned. In this case, you may be entitled to extra benefits to compensate for that difference.

The Social Security Administration provides Social Security Disability Insurance or SSDI. Your eligibility is based on your work history. The SSDI program benefits you and certain family members if you are "insured." Insured means you worked long enough and recently enough and paid Social Security taxes on your earnings. You can qualify for SSDI if you cannot work and engage in a substantial gainful activity because of your medical condition. If you cannot do your previous work or adjust to other work, you may qualify for SSDI. To qualify for SSDI, your illness is expected to last for at least one year or to result in your death. While some programs such as private disability insurance or Workers' Compensation give money to people with partial or short-term disability, SSDI does not.

The Social Security Administration also provides Supplemental Security Income or SSI. To get SSI, you must be disabled, blind, or at least 65 years old and have "limited" income and resources or have a qualifying disability. You must be either a U.S. citizen, a national, or a noncitizen in one of the certain alien classifications the Department of Homeland Security has granted. You must reside in one of the 50 States, the District of Columbia, or the Northern Mariana Islands and be present in the U.S. for an entire calendar month or 30 consecutive days. Children with disabilities or who are blind may also qualify for

SSI. Many people eligible for SSI may also be entitled to regular Social Security benefits. The SSI application is the same one used for standard Social Security benefits.

However, SSI and Social Security are two different programs. Unlike Social Security benefits, SSI benefits are not based on your prior work or a family member's prior work history. In most states, SSI recipients can also get medical assistance or Medicaid to pay for hospital stays, doctor bills, prescription drugs, and other health costs. Many states also provide a supplemental payment to specific SSI recipients. SSI recipients may also be eligible for food assistance.

*Thoughts* - Disability insurance is the forgotten insurance, even though we have a higher probability of being disabled during our work lives than we do of dying. For that reason alone, consider obtaining disability insurance a priority in your budget to protect you and your family. Most disability insurance programs will cover a large portion of your monthly budget, but generally not all. For this reason, if you rely on disability insurance, you may still have to cut back on your expenses to make ends meet. There are some cases where you can purchase additional supplemental disability insurance on top of your regular disability insurance that can pay you up to 100% of income lost.

If you are disabled, over age 59.5, and most of your income is tax-free from your disability payments, consider converting some pre-tax money to post-tax accounts. Since you are in a lower tax bracket because your earnings are tax-free, you may want to convert some pre-tax traditional 401K/IRA money to a post-tax Roth 401K/IRA account. I find that many people on disability and over age 59.5 do not take advantage of being in a lower tax bracket to convert pre-tax money.

The formula for deciding how much disability insurance you need is the same as determining life insurance. Take your income and subtract any taxes; that is the income you need to replace to have the same purchasing power.

# Chapter 7

## Inflation

P*urpose* - Inflation can be defined as the overall general upward price movement of goods and services in a healthy economy.

*Highlights* - To understand finances, you need to understand inflation and how it affects everything we do. Do not consider inflation a bad thing; it is just the way our economy is designed. Pay raises you may get each year are generally set up to help offset that inflation.

The United States economy is designed for prices to increase slightly each year; thus, our dollar devalues a small fraction each day. The Federal Reserve's long-range goal has two mandates: Maximum Sustainable Employment and Price Stability.

Maximum Sustainable Employment is a measurement taken by a wide range of labor market indicators to try and maintain long-range unemployment near 4.1% annually. The annual unemployment rate can change depending on market conditions and is more difficult to measure than the inflation rate.

For Price Stability, the Federal Reserve tries to maintain a 2% annual inflation rate as measured by the Price Index for Personal Consumption Expenditures or PCE. If the annual inflation rate is running ahead of its 2% target, the Federal Reserve can raise the Fed Funds Rate to slow down the economy, thus bringing down inflation, at least in theory. The opposite is also true, and the Fed can lower the interest rate to jumpstart or improve the economy.

Food and energy are excluded when measuring core inflation since they are more volatile and can produce larger fluctuations. By excluding these two commodities, as well as seasonal and temporary products, the Federal Reserve can get a more stable indication of the current inflation rate.

Inflation can hurt our purchasing power. If inflation rises 4% in a year and we get only a 3% cost of living adjustment or COLA, then we lose 1% purchasing power. On the other hand, if inflation rises 4% and we get a 5% COLA, we increase our purchasing power by 1%. Over time, it is crucial that we maintain purchasing power, as failing to do so can put a strain on our budget.

High or rapidly rising inflation can lead to the consumer being unable to afford products or services. In addition, our annual pay raises may not be able to keep up with rising inflation. In such a case, the Federal Reserve will likely hike interest rates to "cool off" the economy and discourage borrowing and spending.

We would not need an annual pay raise or COLA if inflation remained at zero. A near-zero inflation rate environment would indicate a stagnant or stationary economy, typically with slowed production and high unemployment.

Deflation or falling prices is not an ideal situation either. If prices fall, customers will delay purchasing those products in hopes that they will be cheaper at a later date, thus slowing economic activity. In such a case, the Federal Reserve will try to maintain interest rates as low as possible to encourage borrowing and spending to boost the economy.

*Thoughts* - Many people complain about the dollar losing its value, but our economy was designed for the dollar to lose a tiny bit of value each day.

It is essential to know the current inflation rate for your investments. I like to use the Consumer Price Index - Urban Wage Earners and Clerical Workers or CPI-W. For the most part, many workers have a vague idea if their pay raises are keeping up with inflation. Longevity and promotional pay raises should get us ahead of the current inflation rate and increase our purchasing power. In some years, our annual pay raises may fall behind the inflation rate, thus causing us to decrease our spending. If your yearly pay raise is above the current inflation rate, consider increasing your investments with any extra money or possibly increasing your spending if you had to cut back when your pay raises came up short of the inflation rate. Also, remember to increase your budget each year by the current inflation rate, or you will start to find yourself out of money before your next paycheck.

You must also keep track of the year-over-year inflation rate to ensure your investments are not losing purchasing power. Most of the time, our long-range investments are invested in the stock market and will be able to beat inflation over time. However, it may be challenging to outperform rapidly rising inflation, even in the stock market. Sometimes, it is hard to beat inflation in our short-term accounts like an emergency savings account. You may require higher returns to get ahead of inflation, but your options may be limited. In this case, you just need to get the best return for your emergency savings and hope your longer-term investments can compensate for any purchasing power your short-term finances may lose. I would not invest my emergency savings in the stock market. This action will defeat the purpose of your emergency savings, which I will discuss next.

# Chapter 8

Emergency Savings

P*urpose* - Emergency savings are cash reserves set aside for unplanned expenses or financial emergencies.

*Highlights* - Some common examples an emergency fund can be used for include car repairs, home repairs, medical bills, or a loss of income. Generally, most financial advisers recommend setting aside 3 to 6 months of living expenses in an emergency account. Then the next question is how much money should you set aside in an emergency fund? Calculating all your mandatory bills, like mortgage, insurance, utilities, food, etc., is the best way to determine how much you will need for this fund. Remember, you should not include monthly items you do not need, like yoga lessons, cable TV, etc. Just total the bare minimum or the basic necessities to keep you alive. Once you have this number, multiply it by the number of months you want to have in your emergency fund. I personally like to have six months' worth of emergency savings, but if you are short, you may need to build up your fund over time until you are comfortable with the amount. If you need $4,000 per month for the bare necessities, you will need an emergency savings fund of $12,000 for three months and $24,000 for six months. Remember, this money is for the basics only for you to get by in an emergency.

Consider using your emergency fund for any expenses that inhibit you from doing your job or cost income. If your car breaks down and you cannot work and get paid, this is a perfect example of what an emergency fund should be used for. Even a minor financial shock can set you back without an emergency savings account. Research suggests that individuals who do not have an emergency savings account may rely on credit cards or loans, which can lead to debt with very high interest rates. Without an emergency fund, you may be forced to pull from other investments, like retirement funds, which can lead to a penalty if you must cover any unexpected costs.

If you are short on your emergency fund, then start with a plan to add money to this fund until you hit your goal. Even if you can add only $50 each month towards your emergency fund, this will help, and eventually, when you hit your goal, you'll be glad you did.

If your expenses increase over time, you need to increase your emergency savings fund to equal the recommended six months.

*Thoughts* - You always need to treat your emergency savings as an investment. As mentioned above, inflation will eat away at this fund's purchasing power if you earn less interest than the current inflation rate. However, since this fund is for emergencies only, you will need to ensure you keep all principal as you will need this money to last you for six months. With that in mind, your investment options will be limited and should be very conservative to avoid losing your original $24,000. For the most part, you will have only four investment options: your local bank's savings account, a Certificate of Deposit (CD) through your bank or other financial institution, Money Market mutual funds through your local bank or other financial institution, and Treasury bills (T-bills) through TreasuryDirect.gov.

First, ensure you have at least two months' worth of emergency savings available that you can get your hands on within an hour or, in this case, $8,000. This $8,000 will need to be in your local bank or credit union and most likely in a savings account, earning whatever you can get. Generally, savings accounts pay less interest than CDs, Money Markets, or Treasury bills. If your bank offers a Money Market rate higher than their savings rate, select the Money Market account. Savings and

Money Market funds do not penalize you for withdrawing your money, but with CDs or Treasury bills you could lose some interest. Remember, you might lose purchasing power on this $8,000 if the savings or Money Market rate pays less than the current inflation rate. That is okay, as you can make up the difference with the other four months of your emergency savings fund.

Once you have the first $8,000 earning income, you can concentrate on what to do with the remaining $16,000. Since you should need this money only in months two through six, that gives you more options. Most banks and financial institutions will sell you CDs. You may have to pay a penalty for cashing out of a CD early with a local bank or credit union. Sometimes, the penalty can quickly wipe out all your earnings on a CD. A financial institution usually will not charge a penalty for early CD withdrawal. Still, you will probably have to sell the CD on the secondary market at the current rate. Depending on the current interest rates, you may lose or make money on this transaction. Generally, the minimum length of a CD contract is three months. In this case, a CD may not work as you will need some money within two months after you use the first $8,000.

You can look at other financial institutions like Fidelity or Vanguard and try to get a Money Market mutual fund that might pay more than your local bank's Money Market. Usually, larger financial institutions will pay more than local banks due to the volume of money they handle. You may have to link your bank account to the financial institution you want to use to do this option. Generally, transferring your money from a financial institution to your local bank takes only a couple of business days. Once your bank is linked, you just go to the financial institution's website and transfer the funds from (or to) your bank with a couple of clicks. If you choose not to do this option, then you can link your bank account to the government and buy Treasury bills straight from the government at TreasuryDirect.gov.

The government sells Treasury bills in ranges of 4, 8, 13, 17, 26, and 52 weeks. In this case, you could buy Treasuries in the 4, 8, or 13-week range. With your remaining $16,000, you could split this up and buy $8,000 in Treasury bills with a maturity of 8 weeks and the other $8,000 with a maturity of 13 weeks. Another bonus is that government Treasuries are tax-free from state income tax. This type of laddering Treasury bills will allow you to earn more interest than your local bank or credit union might pay and may provide a better chance to beat inflation.

# Chapter 9

## Home Ownership and Investment Property

P*urpose* - Home ownership can be an investment and provide freedom and stability for you and your family.

*Highlights* - Should you rent or should you buy a home? I had to rent for ten years early in life because my budget was so upside down I did not have any money for a down payment for a house. There is nothing wrong with renting an apartment or home. Both renting and home ownership, first and foremost, will provide a roof over your head.

Generally, renting is more affordable and comes with only some of the responsibilities and headaches that can come with owning a home. The apartment complex or homeowner will handle almost all your maintenance. Not having to worry about repairs can be beneficial if you do not have the skills or time to fix any problems that may pop up.

Renting offers flexibility, allowing you to move after your lease is up and not be dependent on a buyer purchasing the property. When renting, the owner may pay some bills, including homeowners' insurance, property taxes, maintenance care, trash collection, water, sewer, and pest control. Not having to pay these bills can save you considerable money over time. You will likely have to purchase renters' insurance to cover your belongings. There are some downsides to renting: you do not get a tax benefit when renting, and your rent can go up whenever your lease is due. In addition, you may have a landlord who does not respond to your concerns about the property.

The great American dream is to buy a home. Home ownership provides stability for you and your family, and you can build home equity over time and take some tax deductions from the interest and property taxes paid. However, saving up enough money for the down payment on a house may take time. You should expect home ownership to cost more than renting, so ensure you have some emergency savings for any unexpected costs. Unlike renting, home ownership may come with a fixed mortgage payment for the life of the loan. One downside to owning a home is that you are now responsible for any repairs and maintenance costs to the property.

Sometimes, there is a misconception that you will always make money when selling a home. That is not always the case. In past years, I have owned two houses that I sold for precisely what I purchased them for years earlier. Whether you make money on the home depends on the current market conditions when you decide to sell. Too many people get caught up in stories of people making tons of money on their houses when they sell them.

When buying a home, you should not just look at the reward, but analyze the risk too. We usually look at the risk subconsciously by driving through the neighborhood. Is the property in a nice subdivision? How are the schools surrounding the property? What about any crime in the community? These are valid risk management concerns when buying a house. Take some time, study the area, and get as much information as you can before purchasing.

Most mortgage companies require that you put down 20% of the loan value to have some equity in the game. If you cannot put down 20%, you may have to apply for Private Mortgage Insurance or PMI. PMI is an insurance program to protect mortgage lenders if a borrower defaults. PMI may cost you between .5% to 1.5% of the loan value and will increase your mortgage payment a little. You can cancel PMI when your primary mortgage loan is below 80% of the original loan value. If you are a veteran, you may qualify for a Veterans Administration or VA loan that does not require you to put down 20% on the purchase of a home.

When you sell your primary residence, you will be exempt from capital gains taxes on the first $250,000 for a single person and $500,000 for a married couple. You can use this exemption only once every two years. You're eligible for the exclusion if you have owned and used your home as your main home for a period aggregating at least two years out of the five years prior to its date of sale. You can meet the ownership and use tests during different 2-year periods. However, you must meet both tests during the 5-year period ending on the date of the sale. Generally, you're not eligible for the exclusion if you excluded the gain from the sale of another home during the two-year period prior to the sale of your home.

Also be sure to keep track of the cost basis on your home. The cost basis is the original price of the property plus any significant improvements you make throughout owning that property. When you sell the property, your profit will be the selling price after fees minus your cost basis.

When buying investment property, do your homework, even more than when buying a home for yourself. You will need to decide if you want to invest in commercial or residential property. Your first task should be to get a professional to help you purchase the property and guide you in renting or leasing your investment.

Some aspects of investment property will be the same as buying a home, such as obtaining a loan, title searches, and the type of location you desire. Differences include the possibility of hiring a property management service to collect the rent, handle any maintenance issues, and work with the renters directly. Property managers will charge you a fee, which will cut into your profit, but can also alleviate many headaches, as they will now take late-night calls when something breaks.

If you are new to investment property, you should concentrate on a condominium or single-family home. Tri- and multi-plex types of homes can be larger purchases and cause more headaches than you initially want to start with. If concentrating on commercial real estate, you may need a lawyer and accountant to help you with all the local regulations and taxes.

The biggest reason people buy investment property is for the additional income and the possibility of the property's appreciation. Make sure you are charging enough rent to pay for all your expenses and still make a profit. One advantage of investing in property is that you can depreciate it. Most residential investment properties can be depreciated over 27.5 years. Realize that you will have to pay capital gains and possibly a depreciation recapture tax when you sell the property.

*Thoughts* - The cost of owning a home will generally be higher than renting, even if your payments on the home are lower than rent. I have heard many stories where people say they bought their house for XX amount and then sold the property five years later for XX amount and made over $XXX,XXX in profit. They forget to tell you all the costs they spent in those five years to maintain, improve, or fix up the property. If you added up all those costs, the profit would be less spectacular.

A rule of thumb that many investors use for buying an investment property is to pay no more than 12 times the annual rent you can charge. For example, if you expect to earn approximately $2000 per month in rent or $24,000 per year, then pay at most $288,000 for the property.

Everybody will have a different experience when buying a house or property. I purchased my first home in California while stationed in Taif, Saudi Arabia. Before leaving, my wife and I were looking for a new home. We searched extensively but had no luck as I headed out the door. I told her if she found anything she liked, buy it. A few days after I arrived in Taif, she called. She had the perfect home in a great neighborhood but needed my signature on all the documents. At the time, we did not have the internet, so she faxed all the documents to Taif for me to sign. We set up two fax machines, one to receive the fax and one to transmit it back to my wife. In those days, the fax paper was one continuous sheet. As soon as the fax came out, I signed where an X was and fed the paper into the second machine. I didn't have time to read any of the pages and assumed my wife had done that. The entire process was completed ten minutes later, and we had a new house. It was the easiest house I ever bought.

I built my next house, which was one of the most stressful experiences I have ever been through. If you go down this road, stay focused on the project, and don't let it overwhelm you and your spouse.

# Chapter 10

Individual Retirement Accounts – IRAs

P*urpose* - An Individual Retirement Account or IRA is a vehicle that allows individuals and their spouses to contribute money to a retirement account.

*Highlights* - An IRA is one of the most popular retirement savings programs for investors. IRAs are available through investment companies, brokerage firms, and banks. To contribute to an IRA, you or your spouse must have earned income such as wages, bonuses, salaries, or income from being self-employed. For example, by earning $75,000 annually, you can contribute to your IRA and your spouse's IRA even if your spouse does not work nor has any wages. You can still participate in an IRA even if your employer has a 401K plan. With an IRA, you can invest in various investment options like mutual funds, exchange-traded funds (ETFs), stocks, bonds, etc. There are four types of IRAs: Traditional IRAs, Roth IRAs, SIMPLE IRAs, and SEP IRAs.

Traditional IRAs have no income limits for contributions. Money in a Traditional IRA will grow tax-deferred until you withdraw it. Traditional IRAs are subject to the Minimum Required Distribution rules. Traditional IRAs are either tax-deductible, partially tax-deductible, or not tax-deductible.

Tax deductible Traditional IRAs will let you take a tax deduction for your contributions. For 2025, the Traditional IRA contribution limits are $7,000 for individuals and an extra $1,000 for participants aged 50 and older. You can deduct all or part of your contributions if you are below the IRS income limits. These limits change each year, so you must keep track of them. Usually, an income tax program can calculate your deduction if you have one after providing all your information. Being able to deduct your IRA contributions from your taxes will also depend on whether you have an employer retirement plan.

You can contribute to a non-deductible Traditional IRA only if you earn over the IRS deductible limits. Even if you are not over the IRS limits, you can still choose to contribute to a non-deductible Traditional IRA. Your contributions will be taxed, and you will maintain a cost basis in the plan for the amount of your contributions. However, your earnings will grow tax-deferred and will be taxed upon withdrawal.

Roth IRAs let you contribute after-tax money into the plan and will grow tax-free. The Roth IRA has the same contribution limits as the Traditional IRA of $7,000 for 2025 and an extra $1,000 for participants aged 50 and over. A single person earning less than $150,000 in 2025 and a married person filing jointly, earning less than $236,000, can contribute the full amount to their Roth IRA. Above these limits, the Roth IRA contribution is phased out. A participant is not eligible to contribute to a Roth IRA in 2025 if filing singly and over $165,000, or married filing jointly over $246,000. Roth IRAs are not subject to Minimum Required Distributions and may be transferred to your heirs through an Inherited Roth IRA.

SIMPLE IRAs are a cheaper version of the more expensive 401K plan, which I will discuss in the next topic. Both employers and their employees can participate. Employers must contribute 2% of the participant's annual salary or match a participant's contributions up to 3%. An employer can match a minimum of 1% for 2 out of 5 years. You must contribute to receive any matching funds in a SIMPLE IRA. For 2025, the contribution for a SIMPLE IRA is $16,500. For participants age 50-59 and 64-65 you may contribute up to an additional $3,500. For participants who have reached ages 60, 61, 62 or 63, the new catch-up contribution limit is increased to the greater of $5,000 or 150% of the regular age 50 catch-up contribution limits for SIMPLE IRA plans in 2025. SIMPLE IRA contributions are not tax deductible as Traditional IRAs are. SIMPLE IRAs are subject to Minimum Required Distribution rules.

SEP IRAs are IRAs for those who are self-employed, owners of a business, or freelancers. Employers can contribute up to 25% of the employee's compensation for a maximum of $70,000 for 2025. If you are self-employed, you may be limited to contributing only up to 20% of your net income. SEP IRA contributions are not tax-deductible for the employees but are tax-deductible for the employer as an expense. SEP IRAs are subject to Minimum Required Distribution rules.

You may have to pay a penalty if you withdraw money from a Traditional, SIMPLE, or SEP IRA before age 59.5. Exceptions to this penalty are listed under IRS 72(t) rules. Those exceptions include hardships such as death and disability, funeral expenses, first-time home buyers, higher education bills, or taking substantially equal periodic payments.

Withdrawals from Roth IRAs must follow the five-year rule where you can withdraw any earnings tax-free only after five years since your first contribution to your Roth IRA account. This rule even applies if you are over age 59.5.

*Thoughts* - I highly recommend participating in an IRA. If your employer does not have a 401K, SEP, or SIMPLE IRA plan, then the IRA may be the only retirement plan you are eligible for, with the exception of Social Security.

If you can invest only a certain amount, then you may have to prioritize where you want your investments to go. If your company has a matching 401K program, then make sure you fund that first, as that is free money from your employer, and then any money left over can be used to fund your IRAs.

If you are a high-income earner and above the legal limits to contribute to a Roth IRA, you might be able to do a "back door Roth IRA conversion." First, you must contribute to a Traditional non-deductible IRA and then convert that money to a Roth IRA. For example, you contribute $5,000 to a Traditional IRA with after-tax funds. After a month, your account grows to $5,100, and you decide to convert all this money to a Roth IRA. Since you have already paid taxes on the original $5,000, you will owe taxes only on the $100 earnings you made in the account before the conversion. Once converted to the Roth structure, the entire $5,100 will grow tax-free along with any gains.

There is a pro-rata rule that prohibits you from picking only after-tax contributions from a Traditional IRA to convert to a Roth IRA. For example, if in your Traditional IRA account, 50% of your balance was funded with pre-tax money and the other 50% was funded with post-tax money, when you convert this money, you cannot just convert the post-tax money and pay no taxes. You will have to convert 50% of the pre-tax and 50% of the post-tax to the Roth. In this scenario, you will owe taxes on the 50% pre-tax conversion. With pro-rata rules, you must count all your Traditional IRA accounts. Back door Roth conversion may not be a good deal if, for years, you have contributed to deductible and non-deductible Traditional IRAs where most of your balance in your account is pre-tax.

Many people forget that you can make catch-up contributions at the beginning of the year when you turn 50. If you turn 50 on July 5th, you can begin the catch-up contributions on the previous January 1st before you turn 50.

# Chapter 11

## Workplace Savings – 401K Plans

P*urpose* - A 401K is a Defined Contribution retirement plan allowing employees to contribute part of their wages towards retirement.

*Highlights* - Similar in structure to the IRA, 401Ks may enable you to contribute significantly more than you can in an IRA.

In 2025, the annual contribution limit for a 401K is $23,500. For participants age 50-59 and 64-65 you may contribute up to an additional $7,500. For participants who have reached ages 60, 61, 62 or 63, the new catch-up contribution limit is increased to the greater up to $11,250 instead of $7,500. Some employers may match up to 5% of your salary into the plan.

There are two types of 401K plans. A Traditional 401K allows you to contribute pre-tax money to the plan. These contributions will not count as taxable wages on your W-2. These plans have no income limits, and all employees can participate. Distributions from a Traditional 401K will count as wages for tax purposes. Typically, you can take a distribution at age 59.5 while working or age 55 and retired. Money inside a Traditional 401K must meet the Minimum Required Distribution schedules, which I will discuss later.

The second type of 401K plan is a Roth 401K. Some employers may offer only the Traditional 401K option and not the Roth 401K option. The Roth and the Traditional plans usually operate within the same 401K plan. You can contribute to either a Traditional or Roth 401K or both simultaneously. However, you must stay within the annual contribution limits. For example, you can contribute $10,000 to a Traditional 401K and $13,500 to a Roth 401K for a total of $23,500 below age 50 for 2025. Unlike the Roth IRA, the Roth 401K has no income limits for an employer to be able to participate. Distributions from Roth 401K plans are not taxed if they meet the criteria for qualified distributions. You must hold a Roth 401K account for at least five years to avoid any penalties on gains. Also, a participant must be at least 59.5 years old or 55 and retired to avoid penalties. Minimum Required Distributions are not required for Roth 401K money. Anyone who inherits your Roth 401K will also receive that money tax-free through an Inherited Roth IRA, but they must deplete that account within ten years.

Generally, your 401K plan will have a few dozen mutual funds, possibly company stock, for you to choose from. A mutual fund will consist of many stocks, bonds, other investments, or a combination of all three in one fund. A mutual fund is considered less risky than buying an individual stock or bond since it holds many different investments. When I was involved in overseeing a 401K plan, we set up a "mutual fund style box." This 9-fund style box comprises domestic mutual funds consisting of a Large value, Large blend, Large growth, Medium value, Medium blend, Medium growth, Small value, Small blend, and Small growth. These nine mutual funds usually comprise most of the domestic equity funds available in a 401K plan. In addition, a 401K plan may also have some mutual funds outside of this 9-fund style box. Some 401K plans may contain short, long, and inflation types of bonds, real estate funds, and even some overseas funds. You may also have age-based funds in your plan that correspond to the year you will retire, and as you get closer to that age, these types of funds will become more conservative.

When choosing a mutual fund for a 401K plan, the plan committee will usually look at thousands of mutual funds, narrow them down to a few, and then pick the best one. In most cases, the 401K committee selects the best mutual fund they can find to put in their plans. The funds in the 401K plan are usually called "core funds."

Some 401K plans will allow customers to choose mutual funds outside their core funds, enabling a 401K participant to purchase funds held by another institution. Generally, the fees will be higher when selecting a mutual fund outside the plan but may give the participant more choices.

*Thoughts* - One of the best ways to learn about your 401K plan is in the Summary Plan Description (SPD). The IRS requires the SPD to be readily available for all employees. The SPD will provide information on contribution limits, loans, withdrawals, tax consequences, your rights as a participant, and any other aspects that may affect your 401K plan.

Contributing to a 401K retirement plan is a great way to create wealth. If your employer has a matching program, take full advantage of that option, as the company contributions are free. Your 401K balance will grow over time by consistently contributing to a 401K and benefiting from market returns. Make sure you are well diversified, and if needed, seek financial help to develop a plan.

One issue I saw when overseeing a 401K plan was that many participants thought they could pick better mutual funds than the committee could, so they purchased mutual funds outside the core account. When a participant does this, he leaves the "institutional mutual funds" in the core account and buys "retail mutual funds" with higher fees. A participant will need better performance to compensate for these higher fees to get the same returns available in the core account funds. I saw many reports where participants buying mutual funds outside the plan performed 3% to 4% worse than participants purchasing the core funds within the plan.

If your 401K plan allows it, you can borrow up to 50% of the vested value up to a maximum of $50,000 from your account. Generally, you have up to five years to pay back the loan. You do not have to pay any taxes or penalties for this loan since it is not a withdrawal. However, many plans will let you contribute to your 401K only after the loan is paid in full.

If you have a Roth 401K available, the million-dollar question is, "Should I contribute to the Traditional 401K or the Roth 401K"? To answer that question, you must know the amount of your income at retirement and the future tax rates. Nobody can predict future tax rates, so knowing which option to contribute to would be impossible. Perhaps contribute 50% to the Traditional 401K plan and the other 50% to the Roth 401K. Having a mix of pre-tax and post-tax retirement funds in your accounts is not a bad idea. Contributing to the Traditional and Roth 401K can be used to your tax advantage. For example, you need to withdraw $25,000 from your 401K account to make your yearly budget. You calculate from the current tax brackets that you can withdraw $15,000 and still stay in the 12% tax bracket, but any withdrawals above that will take you into the 22% tax bracket. In a case like this, you may want to withdraw $15,000 of the $25,000 from your Traditional 401K to be taxed at the lower 12% rate and then withdraw the remaining $10,000 tax-free from the Roth 401K. This tax planning will enable you to maximize your investments and minimize your taxes.

Some 401K plans may have an after-tax limit that will enable you to exceed the annual 401K contribution limits. All the money above the contribution limits can be only in after-tax dollars. If your 401K plan has this option and you have the means to take advantage of this program, then you can contribute up to $70,000 in 2025 into your 401K plan. This limit is the maximum amount of money you can contribute to all Defined Contribution Plans. Contributions to the

"Catch-Up" part of your 401K plan do not count against the $69,000 IRS limit. If your plan allows rollovers, you may be able to then rollover any after-tax money into a Roth IRA without any tax consequences. These rollovers can be on top of any annual contribution limits to your IRAs.

Under the IRS 72(t) rules, you can withdraw money from your 401K account early without penalty for hardships such as death and disability, funeral expenses, first-time home buyers, higher education bills, or by taking equal periodic payments.

If your 401K plan allows it, after your retirement, you may be able to leave your funds in your employer's plan until you spend it or until your death. However, Traditional 401K funds may have to be converted under the Minimum Required Distribution rules. If your employer allows in-plan conversions, you can convert any Traditional 401K contributions to the Roth 401K plan. You will have to pay taxes on any pre-tax monies unless used for Charitable Qualified Distributions or QCDs, which I will discuss later.

# Chapter 12

## Precious Metals

P*urpose* - Owning precious metals can protect your investments against inflation, weakening of currency, or even economic collapse.

*Highlights* - Gold and Silver have existed for thousands of years and have held value since Biblical times.

Gold and Silver are seen as a hedge against inflation. When an economy experiences high inflation, investors purchase gold and silver, believing their prices will increase, thus protecting some of their assets. In some years, you may see rising inflation, which can put upward pressure on precious metals, and a strong U.S. dollar, which can put downward pressure on precious metals. In a situation like this, the price of precious metals can be very volatile.

Also, gold and silver prices usually increase when investors lose confidence in their currency. Since gold and silver are valued based on the U.S. dollar, when the dollar's value declines against other world currencies, it can put upward pressure on gold and silver, thus increasing demand and price. As mentioned in the inflation chapter, the Federal Reserve is mandated to maintain inflation by approximately 2% annually. With a 2% inflation rate, the U.S. dollar devalues each day, and in reality, precious metals should increase in price slightly each day since they are priced in U.S. dollars.

People also tend to invest in gold and silver when global economic uncertainties increase. They are considered safer assets than stocks or bonds in uncertain times. During these times, gold and silver may experience significant price increases.

Supply and demand can also determine the price of precious metals. If supply is down, demand will probably increase, causing the prices to increase, and vice versa, when supply is up, the price may decline. Precious metals are also used for industrial purposes, such as in semiconductors, solar panels, medical devices, phones, automobiles, and other everyday items we use. These uses can sometimes add to the value of precious metals.

*Thoughts* - It is essential to maintain portfolio diversification. Many financial advisors recommend keeping some precious metals in your portfolio. Years ago, holding at least 10% of your investment portfolio in precious metals was recommended for asset protection. This sentiment has waned over the years, with people holding less than 10% in their portfolios today.

If you want to invest in precious metals, the cheapest and easiest way is through mutual funds and exchange-traded funds (ETFs). The expenses to get started in these funds will be minimal compared to purchasing the metals outright. You can buy mining stocks on the exchanges or trade options or futures. If you want to trade precious metals regularly, I recommend purchasing a mutual fund or ETF.

Should you buy actual gold and silver bullion? You sure can, but there are a couple of problems with this. First, if you purchase actual gold coins and bars, you will have to pay a premium for those purchases. For gold, the current premium to buy is approximately $60 for one ounce of gold. For example, if gold is $2,000, you can expect to pay a total with the premium of $2,060. The price of gold will have to increase from $2,000 to $2,060 for you to break even on this purchase. At the time of this writing, silver had a premium of $1.50 for one ounce. If you buy rare gold and silver coins, expect the premiums to be considerably higher. People who purchase actual bars and coins generally plan to keep them for extended periods in case of uncertainty in the future.

The second problem with purchasing gold and silver bullion or coins is where and how to store them. You can pick up a safe and keep it in your house or in a secure facility. It may be beneficial to ensure the safe has some fire protection in case your home burns down so you do not lose your investment and possibly your important papers. Another option is to get a safety deposit box at your local bank, which is usually reasonably priced.

You cannot purchase actual precious metals in a regular IRA. You will need to use a self-directed IRA to be able to invest in actual bullion or coins. You must follow the IRS guidelines and buy from an approved dealer. Your precious metals will need to be stored in an IRS-approved depository. The same IRS withdrawal rules apply to regular IRAs. When you are age 59.5, you may request that your actual bullion or coins be shipped to you, or you may sell them and take the cash proceeds instead.

To purchase precious metals online, ensure the facility is reputable and the prices align with other dealers. If the dealer will not repurchase your precious metals when you are ready to sell, that is a red flag in my book. You can also buy and sell on eBay or Facebook marketplace, but again, make sure you are purchasing or selling to a reputable business or individual. The price of gold and silver has always held some value for thousands of years and will likely continue to do so.

# Chapter 13

Risk Management

Purpose - Risk management analyzes the risks associated with your financial decisions and protects you from losses.

*Highlights* - Risk is defined as a hazard, a peril, or exposure to loss or injury and refers to the chance that some unfavorable event will occur. There are two parts to all investments: risk and return. So, how do you measure risk for an investment? You probably already measure risks in some of your financial decisions yet do not realize it. When buying a house, the first thing we consider is location, location, location. Analyzing where to buy your home is a risk analysis assessment, pure and simple. When buying a car, we may look at Consumer Reports on the reliability of that car, which is another risk assessment. So why is it that when we buy mutual funds or stocks, we are not sure what risk measurements to use? Investment firms usually do not offer much help since they will send you a prospectus that lists the returns for their stocks or mutual funds but little information about the risk of that investment. The prospectus may indicate that a mutual fund has less or more risk than the benchmark, but how risky is the benchmark?

If you participate in a 401K plan, the administrators will have a fiduciary responsibility to do a risk analysis of the mutual funds they hold in their plan. They may use risk measurements like Beta, Sharpe Ratio, Sortino Ratio, Treynor Ratio, Upside/Downside Capture Ratio, or a combination of these. I will not cover these risk management measurements as they are outside the scope of this book. Instead, I will focus on a simple risk calculation when comparing several mutual funds from the same asset class.

To understand risk analysis, you need to keep it simple. I like to use standard deviation as my "go-to" risk measurement. Standard deviation is the measure of the dispersion relative to its mean. Standard deviation measures the volatility of Fund X only and does not care about other mutual funds, including Fund X's benchmark. Think of standard deviation like a dart board. The farther away from the middle you throw the dart, the greater the risk the dart will not hit any numbers. Standard deviation measures Fund X's annual rate of returns over a specific number of years to determine Fund X's dispersion. The more spread out those yearly rates of return are, the higher the standard deviation or risk will be.

For example, say we want to measure Fund X's risk against its benchmark, the S&P 500. Fund X has a 15-year standard deviation of 15, and the S&P 500 has a 15-year standard deviation of 18. In this case, the S&P 500 has approximately 17% more volatility or risk than Fund X over the last 15 years. Does this mean we should invest in Fund X? Not yet, as we only have the risk picture of our risk versus reward equation. We must look at returns for the reward or performance comparison over the same time frame. Using our example, over the last 15 years, Fund X has a yearly average return of 10%, while the S&P 500 has a yearly average return of 11%. In this case, the S&P 500 outperforms Fund X by 10% annually. Doing these calculations in your head can get complicated, which is a reason many people do not measure risk. To recap, Fund X has 17% less risk and 10% less return than the S&P 500. You will need a calculator to determine how much return you get for 1 unit of risk. First, I will calculate Fund X's return by its standard deviation (10%/15 = .66%). In this case, for 1 unit of risk, Fund X has a .66% return. For the S&P 500 (11%/18 = .61%), the S&P 500 has a .61% return for 1 unit of risk. This simple calculation tells us that on a risk-adjusted basis, Fund X has a slightly better return: .66% versus .61%.

Remember, when using this simple standard deviation measurement, you must compare mutual funds or stocks in the same asset class. Do not use this type of measurement to compare a bond mutual fund with a stock mutual fund, as it is like comparing apples to oranges. Use this simple measurement to compare a mutual fund or a stock to its benchmark.

Does this mean we should invest in Fund X over the S&P 500? To answer that question, we need to look at the four possibilities. If Fund X had less risk and better returns, this would be a good choice, and I would invest in this fund. I might invest in this fund if Fund X has more risk and a better return. I might invest in this fund if Fund X has less risk and less return. I would not invest in this fund if Fund X has more risk and less return. Your goal is to try and find a mutual fund or stock with less risk and better returns than its benchmark.

*Thoughts* - In the movie Field of Dreams, the voice says, "If you build it, they will come." I think of risk management as "If you control your risk, the returns will come." For this reason, I make risk analysis the primary decision in my investment choices. You need to control the roller coaster ride in the financial markets, and believe me, there will be some wild rides. When you are younger, you can afford the wild ups and downs of the market since you have more time to recover. You will value a smoother roller coaster ride with your investments when you get older.

Make a conscious effort to analyze the risk of all financial decisions, whether big or small. This effort will help you make an informed decision.

Many investors believe you must pick mutual funds with the lowest fees or select only index funds. This approach to picking funds is not a risk management strategy. Mutual Fund fees are already deducted from their Net Asset Value or NAV as required by the Securities and

Exchange Commission. The NAV is calculated by subtracting the mutual fund's liabilities from the value of all its shares and dividing that by the number of shares it has issued. As shown above, the fees have already been deducted from the returns. Mutual funds with low fees may have high volatility, so be sure to analyze their standard deviation.

Can an investor find a mutual fund or stock that can beat its index in performance? Sure, but a fund or stock that also has less risk than its index is harder to find. Nobody said investing was going to be easy. Look at both the risk and the return pieces of the puzzle to get the complete picture.

# Chapter 14

Financial Advisors

P*urpose* - Financial advisors can help guide you with your financial goals and answer any questions you or your spouse may have.

*Highlights* - Today, there are two types of financial advisors: robo-advisors and traditional advisors. Each one can help with financial goals, although with some differences.

Robo-advisors or digital advisors are new to the financial scene and use mathematical equations and algorithms to give you a financial plan based on your inputs. Robo advisors will accept clients with little money and usually charge a fee based on how many assets they manage. This fee can range from .25% to .50% of Assets Under Management (AUM).

A robo-advisor will set up an online investment platform for you, and you can navigate all your investments from one place. Initially, a robo-advisor will ask for your goals, risk tolerance, and length of time for investment. After collecting all this information, the automated financial program will recommend a mix of assets to you and then rebalance each year to ensure you are on the path to your selected goals. Robo-advisors can benefit couples who are new to investing but have little money or knowledge about investing. However, robo-advisors can take the personal touch out of financial advice and may leave you with unanswered questions. Also, if you are an active trader and plan on buying and selling regularly, a robo-advisor might not be a good fit, as their programming usually takes a long-term approach.

Traditional advisors can offer personalized advice and answer any questions you may have. They can also advise you on estate planning, tax planning, and some of the more complicated aspects of the financial industry. Traditional advisors will generally cost more than a robo-advisor and may require a higher balance to use their services.

Traditional advisors usually charge their clients either fee-based, AUM-based, or commission-based fees for their services. Fee-based advisors can charge for the entire year or a one-time visit. The first visit to a financial advisor is usually free and will determine if that advisor is a good fit for you. Fee-based charges for managing your portfolio can range from $1,000 to $8,000 a year. AUM-based fees typically range from .5% to 2% of the assets the financial advisor manages. For example, if the advisor manages $1,000,000 of your investments and charges a 1% yearly fee, then you can expect to pay the financial advisor or their firm $10,000 annually. Traditional advisors may also charge based on commissions. This type of fee can vary based on the amount of trades you execute or the products you want to invest in. If you are a frequent stock or mutual fund trader, this fee structure can add up fast and may not be your best option.

*Thoughts* - Do not be afraid to speak to a financial advisor. They are ordinary people, just like you and me. Sometimes, we may be hesitant because we do not have an extensive portfolio or are having budgeting issues and are afraid to bring those issues up to a financial planner. Everybody has had ups and downs in their financial matters over the years. Most financial advisors are glad to meet with you and explain the financial programs they may offer without any commitment from you. If you do not know any financial advisors, ask friends and family if they have any advisors they may recommend. I recommend interviewing at least three financial advisors before deciding who you want to invest your money with. After all, the advisor will control your nest egg and may determine if you get to retire when you want. If you choose to go with a financial planner, you can do a trial run and let him or her handle a small percentage of your portfolio to see the results. If satisfied, then you can add to that percentage.

When considering financial advisors, find out if they have a fiduciary responsibility for you. Fiduciary responsibility means they will act in your best interest instead of their own or the firm they work for. Also, make sure they are a Certified Financial Planner or CFP. A CFP must have several years of experience in the financial field and pass the CFP exam. They must adhere to a high ethical standard when handling your finances. Also, ensure any brokerage firms your financial advisor wants to use are members of the Securities Investor Protection Corporation (SIPC). In the unlikely event they become insolvent, you may have some protection to recover some of your investments.

Financial advisors can provide you with resources that might not be available to the average investor. They can look at your overall picture and help you with insurance, estate planning, long-term care, and any other long-range financial products you may want. A financial advisor makes money by selling you advice, so be aware of the associated costs.

Having some financial understanding before talking to a financial advisor is best. Sometimes, people, including myself, need help understanding every aspect of all the financial products offered. If you need help understanding what the advisor is saying, then stop and ask. If he or she explains it again and you still don't understand, ask for information in layperson's terms. Do not be embarrassed. Ensure you fully understand the products and the costs before making any agreements. Remember, financial advisors are trained to know these subjects; you are probably not. If the advisor ever becomes frustrated with you for not understanding their products or costs, that is a red flag, and I would find another advisor.

If an advisor tells you an investment product is 100% guaranteed, that is also a red flag in my book, and I would find another advisor. There are no guarantees in the investment world; not even U.S. government bonds are 100% guaranteed.

# Chapter 15

529 College Savings and Prepaid Tuition Plans

P*urpose* - The IRS-regulated 529 plans enable earnings to grow tax-free if used to pay for a beneficiary's schooling.

*Highlights* - There are two types of 529 plans: 529 Savings Plans and 529 Prepaid Tuition Plans. The 529 Savings Plan is the most common type. The 529 Prepaid Tuition Plan is available in only 12 states at the time of this writing.

In a 529 Savings Plan, the account owner maintains ownership of the funds and can change the beneficiary at any time, but there are specific rules to follow. The funds must be used for qualified educational expenses: tuition, room and board, textbooks, fees, and some classroom equipment. If used for qualified expenses, withdrawals are not subject to federal or state income taxes. There is a 10% penalty on investment gains if 529 funds are used for non-qualified expenses.

Funds may also be used for private elementary, middle, and high school. However, there is a $10,000 per calendar year limit. There is no limit to using 529 funds for higher education expenses.

As of 2025, the owner of the 529 may transfer any unused 529 funds penalty-free to the beneficiary's Roth IRA. The 529 account must have been open for at least 15 years, and the rollover amount must have been in the account for at least five years. In addition, this program has a lifetime rollover limit of $35,000.

The other type of 529 is the Prepaid Tuition Plan. This plan will let you pay for college tuition at today's prices. For example, this plan will allow you to fund college years before a child will attend at a lower tuition rate. Usually, 529 Prepaid Tuition Plans can be used only in-state or with affiliated schools. The Prepaid Tuition Plan may be a good option if you believe your child will attend a university within that state. With this in mind, the Prepaid Tuition 529 has less flexibility than the 529 Savings Plan. There is also a Private College 529 Prepaid Tuition Plan that works along the same concept, except this plan is designed for private schools across the United States. Hundreds of schools participate in the Private College 529 program.

*Thoughts* - This is an excellent program for a parent or even grandparent to help fund college or private schooling for a child or grandchild. As a grandparent, this can help take the burden off your child in helping to fund your grandchild's education while your children may just be starting in the workforce. You will have to commit regular contributions to fund these accounts, as inflation will increase, causing college tuition to increase every year. As a grandparent, I deposit money for birthdays and Christmas into the grandchild's account.

When selecting mutual funds within the 529, I prefer age-based mutual funds. These funds become more conservative as the child nears college age. There is a case where the owner and the beneficiary might be the same in a 529 account. If an owner wants to start a 529 for a child in the future, he can list himself as the beneficiary and select a more aggressive fund than an age-based fund. Once the child is born, the owner can change the beneficiary to the child and select the age-based fund.

Another great program I have had for years is using my Fidelity Visa credit card to help fund a 529 account. This card does not have an annual fee. Currently, Fidelity pays 2% cash back into the 529 of my choice each month. I encourage all parents or grandparents to use this option to help fund college. With multiple contributors using a credit card for cash back, a 529 account can quickly increase in value. Using this strategy, I was able to pay tuition, room and board, and books for three full years at a major university for a niece.

Some people are attached to their credit cards for airline miles. The problem is that airline miles accumulated stay the same after they are earned, whereas investment in a mutual fund can potentially increase in value. Also, many airlines keep increasing the required miles for a free trip.

Remember to pay off your credit card each month. You do not want to fund one account with cash back but pay interest on the credit card; that would defeat the purpose.

Generally, there are three ways to withdraw funds to pay for qualified expenses with a 529 account. 1) You can transfer money directly to the school from your financial institution holding the 529. 2) You can transfer the money directly to the student's bank and have them pay the associated bill, or 3) You can write a check to the school or the manager of the residence and then reimburse yourself by selling the funds and transferring them to your bank account. No matter which option you choose to pay the bills, keep records of all the bills and transfers of funds for tax purposes. You should save these records: 1) A copy of the bill. 2) A copy of the payment, i.e., a credit card receipt or a copy of the check after it is deposited. 3) A copy of the withdrawal from the 529, which should equal the bill amount. Remember to keep these receipts in a folder in case any tax questions arise later.

# Chapter 16

## Wills

P*urpose* - A Will is a legal document communicating a person's wishes when disposing of their assets at death. A will's format can be written or oral.

*Highlights* - Generally, there are some requirements for you to be able to establish a will. You must be at least 18 years of age. You must be of sound mind and understand the property you own and that you are leaving that property to other individuals, groups, or charities upon your death. You must be able to identify the assets and the beneficiaries of those assets. You must designate an executor, if needed, to handle your instructions listed in the will. Lastly, you must have signatures on the will for it to be valid. The signatures required usually include your signature and two witnesses who are not related to you and are over 18. Each state may have slightly different rules and provide online examples of wills that meet their state requirements.

If you die without a will, the courts in that state will decide what happens to all your possessions. Setting up a will can give you control of your assets and to whom they will be distributed. If you are a parent of young children, then you can designate who will be the guardian of those children in case of your death.

Most wills will have to go through the probate process, but not all. If you have an account that lists a beneficiary, those assets will likely not go through probate. Any property held jointly with rights of survivorship will pass directly to that beneficiary upon your death. Also, if you have a small estate, you may be able to avoid probate or go through a simplified version of probate. You can also avoid probate if you have a surviving dependent or partner who can show transfer of ownership. If your state allows Transfer on Death Deeds, you might be able to skip the probate process on specific properties.

Several items should not be in a will, including life insurance policies, retirement accounts, pension plans, property assigned to a living trust, investment accounts, and bank accounts, as these will generally require beneficiaries to be named.

There are many types of wills, and I will list seven of the most common: A Simple Will lists all of your assets and the beneficiaries whom you want to receive them. You can also list a guardian for any minor children or dependents and an executor to carry out your wishes.

A Joint Will is usually for spouses but is less flexible. A Joint Will defines what both spouses agree to and cannot be changed when one party dies. A Joint Will can create issues if the surviving spouse gets remarried or becomes incapacitated.

A Testamentary Trust Will goes into effect upon your death. This type of will transfers your assets to a trust to be distributed to your designated beneficiaries. People may have some of their assets in a trust while living and, upon death, use a Testamentary Trust Will to move the remaining assets to that trust. A Testamentary Trust Will is great for beneficiaries with special needs or for minor children.

A Living Will concerns your medical care and who you want to make decisions for you in case of incapacitation. It is a legal document that provides instructions for your care and, if needed, for when to be taken off life support.

A Holographic Will is one you prepare in your handwriting. In some states, no witnesses are required. Holographic Wills are not recognized in all states, so check your state's requirements to see if a Holographic Will is valid.

A Video Will is accomplished by using a camera. You can record your wishes by describing or reading your will in front of the camera. A Video Will should be used as a supplement to a written will.

A Deathbed Will is usually drawn up right before death is imminent. It is legally binding and may have errors, causing a higher probability for this type of will to be contested in a court of law. For this reason, it is essential to have a will already completed in case something unexpected happens.

*Thoughts* - Many wills are affordable and can be drafted online, where you have only to fill in the blanks. You need to verify your state's requirements for a will, as each state differs. Wills are the cornerstone of your estate planning and can mitigate family disagreements over your assets upon death. Your wills is most likely to be the presiding document that a probate court will use to determine how to settle your estate. Because of the reasonable price and the ease of writing a will, there are very few reasons for anyone not to have one.

Once you complete a will, get a copy on a disk to make future changes. I usually ask for the will to be converted to a Microsoft Word program to readily adjust any area that might have changed. If you do not have any witnesses available, you can always go to your local bank and have the tellers witness for you. You may need to update a will due to the death of a child, spouse, or parent. Also, if something happens to your named executor, then you will need to change that in your will, too. Sometimes, we think of changes only in our family but forget about any changes to the executor. Include your will in a year-end financial review to ensure no changes are required.

There may be cases when you want to leave a child out of the will for various reasons. Make sure you are specific and list what that child is to receive or not to receive so the courts do not view this as an unintended omission on your part.

When you travel, you and your spouse should leave instructions on where your will is located. You may leave a copy on the coffee table while you are gone, but ensure you have the original will in a safe place. I recommend having your will in a fireproof box, a safe, or even a safety deposit box at your local bank. Leave instructions so your loved ones can find all your estate documents.

If you have underage children or children from a different marriage, you may need a trust over a will to handle expenses well beyond your death. I will cover the various trust options in the next chapter.

# Chapter 17

## Trusts

P*urpose* - A trust is a legal document that gives you, an executor, or an institution the power to manage your assets.

*Highlights* - A trust can be used for many reasons, including medical, charitable, estate, and tax planning. Most trusts will cost more to implement than a will. A will most likely will have to go through the probate courts, whereas a trust does not. Since a trust does not have to go through probate, its assets can be distributed faster without waiting for a court decision.

There are several types of trusts. A Living Trust is set up and funded during your lifetime. Living Trusts can be irrevocable or revocable. With an Irrevocable Living Trust, the assets do not belong to you anymore but to the trust itself. With very few exceptions, you cannot make any changes once an irrevocable trust is set up. The assets may be subject to federal and state taxes but not estate taxes. A Revocable Living Trust will allow you to control the assets in the trust. You can change the trust any time you like or even cancel it altogether.

A Generation-Skipping Trust will enable you to transfer your assets to your grandchildren or great-grandchildren to avoid paying estate taxes. Transfers to your children are not considered generation-skipping. You may have to pay a Generation Skipping Transfer tax (GST) if you go over the lifetime GST tax exemption rate. Check with a tax consultant before setting up this type of trust.

A Qualified Personal Residence Trust can switch your primary or secondary home to a trust and out of your estate. This type of trust can be beneficial for removing some assets from your estate.

A Credit Shelter Trust can pass part of your estate, usually up to the lifetime gift tax, to a trust to avoid estate taxes. When assets are passed to a Credit Shelter Trust, they are free from federal and state taxes after the spouse's death.

A Qualified Terminable Interest Property or QTIP Trust can split some property investments. You can use a QTIP trust if you have children from a previous marriage. For example, if you have income-producing property, you can direct that income to your spouse while he or she is alive, and when he or she dies, the property will pass to your children or another designee.

An Irrevocable Life Insurance Trust lets you put your life insurance into a trust and remove it from your taxable estate. When you die, the life insurance proceeds can be used to pay for any funeral expenses, and the remainder will go to your heirs tax-free. One downside of this trust is that when you transfer the life insurance policy to the trust, you cannot borrow against the insurance policy.

A Special Needs Trust is designed to benefit people with special needs. This type of trust can be used for children or even parents. In some states, this type of trust is called a Supplemental Needs Trust. A Special Needs Trust is an irrevocable trust and will not affect the special needs person's government benefits.

*Thoughts* - A trust can provide many benefits over a will. However, a trust will also cost you more money than a will. If you have minor children, you may want to have a revocable trust with the option to change when your children become adults. If either spouse has children from a previous marriage, an irrevocable trust may be essential to ensure you and your spouse's assets go to their intended beneficiary. If you have adult children who are not mature enough to handle a large sum of money, a trust could disperse your assets over time to them. A trust can guarantee your wishes.

It is best to seek legal advice for any trusts, as each state may have different rules associated with specific trusts. Ensure you get all your questions answered and your assets are distributed according to your wishes. Also, ensure you understand the costs associated with administering a trust.

Some financial advisors use a rule of thumb: Any estate over $100,000 should consider establishing a trust.

# Chapter 18

In Case I Die Letter

P*urpose* - To have an organized letter that lists all your financial accounts and important information in case of your death.

*Highlights* - The "In Case I Die Letter" will encompass almost all of the topics in this book. The letter is a quick overview of your relevant information so a spouse or beneficiaries can access your financial information promptly.

Here are some examples of what I would put into an "In Case I Die Letter" for my spouse. I recommend adding or deleting any information from this list to customize your letter. I divided the actions into two categories: immediate attention and not-so-immediate attention.

*Immediate Attention*

Burial Wishes - We have two plots already paid for at XYZ Cemetery. Their phone number is 1-234-5678. Be sure to get as many copies of my death certificate as possible.

Emergency Savings - We have XYZ amount in our Emergency Savings account. Our account number is 123456. You can use this money for any burial expenses you may incur. When you are ready, you will need to provide a copy of my death certificate and have my name taken off all of our bank accounts. The bank's phone number is 1-234-5678.

Life Insurance - I have XYZ amount of life insurance with my company. Most of this money will be tax-free. You can invest this money in our brokerage account XYZ or use it to pay off the house—your choice. I also have a term life insurance policy with ABC Life Insurance Company for XYZ amount. All of this money will be tax-free. I would invest this money in our brokerage account. ABC Life Insurance Company's phone number is 1-234-5678.

Accidental Death and Dismemberment Insurance - I have an Accidental Death and Dismemberment policy on my life. It is worth ZXY amount and is with ABC Life Insurance Company. Their phone number is 1-234-5678. If I die from an accident, then they will pay the policy amount. If I did not die from an accident, then call them and inform them of my death and cancel the policy. I recommend you put this money into our joint account if I die from an accident.

My Pension - Since I am vested in my company's pension, you will be eligible for a portion of my pension. If we are already drawing my retirement pension, it will continue until you die. If we have not started taking my pension, you will receive the Joint Spousal option for the remainder of your life. You can have this money directly deposited into our bank account. If my company does not reach out to you promptly, call the retirement department at 1-234-5678 and tell them of my death.

*Not-So-Immediate Attention*

Health Insurance - You can still stay on my health insurance plan from the company until you reach age 65. Once you turn 65, you will be eligible for Medicare, and my company's health insurance will end. You can call my company's HR department if you have any questions. Their number is 1-234-5678.

Healthcare Savings Account - We have a Healthcare Savings Account (HSA) we have been contributing to over the years. You will need to transfer this into your name and supply them with a copy of my death certificate. You can use this money to pay for any medical, dental, or vision expenses our health insurance does not cover. If you are on Medicare, you can use this money to pay your Medicare Part B and Part D premiums.

My IRAs - I recommend you transfer all my Roth IRA to your Roth IRA and all my Traditional IRA to your Traditional IRA. You will not incur any taxes on this transfer. You will have to supply a copy of my death certificate. Our investment company's phone number is 1-234-5678, and my account number is 123456. Just add this money to our current investment selections.

My 401K - It may take up to 60 days for all my employer contributions to show up in my 401K account. You will have to send XYZ Financial Company a copy of my death certificate. Once they have this, they can transfer my 401K account to your IRA accounts. Have them transfer my Roth 401K money into your Roth IRA account and my Traditional 401K money into your Traditional IRA account. You should not have to pay any taxes on these transfers. I would add this money to our current investment selections. XYZ Financial Company's phone number is 1-234-5678, and my account number is 123456.

Other investments - Our brokerage account is a joint account, so you will need to remove my name from the account. They will want a copy of my death certificate. XYZ Financial Company's phone number is 1-234-5678, and our account number is 123456.

Our son's 529 account - You will want to transfer ownership of our son's 529 account to yourself. You can call our Investment Company at 123-456-7890 and talk to a representative. You will probably have to send them a copy of my death certificate as well.

Financial Advisor - When you get a chance, visit our financial advisor and see if they have any changes to our plan now that I am deceased. You will need to transfer all my accounts into your name. Our financial advisor can help in this process. They should also help you with any Minimum Required Distributions you must take in the future.

Umbrella Insurance - You can still keep our Umbrella Insurance if you want. It is for XYZ amount and costs ABC amount per year. The paperwork is with our other important documents.

Long-Term Care Insurance - You will need to update our policy and have them remove my name. You should not have to pay any more monthly premiums for me once I am off the policy.

Our Deed on our Home - You will need to update the deed on our house and remove my name from the deed. You can get this form at the county records office. Also, look into filling out a Transfer on Death Deed to transfer our house to our son if you want. This way, our house will avoid probate.

Our Will - You will need to take my name out of our will and update it. The will is located in our fireproof box. You can make the preferred changes on the disk and print out a copy to be signed by you and two witnesses.

Social Security - You can draw your Social Security at age 60 (survivor benefits) or wait until age 67 if you would like. Make sure you file for Social Security three months before wanting your benefits. You can draw Spousal Benefits based on my earnings. You will need to provide a marriage certificate to the Social Security Administration.

Medicare - If you take Social Security before age 65, you will automatically be enrolled in Medicare. If you are eligible for Medicare, you will have to pay for Medicare Part B premiums out of your Social Security check. The deduction is done automatically. If you do not apply for Social Security prior to age 65, enroll in Medicare four months before age 65. You can use the Health Savings Account to pay for any Medicare Part B or D premiums or get reimbursed for those premiums if they are automatically deducted from your Social Security check.

Safety Deposit box, safes, and passwords - We have a safety deposit box at ACD Bank. The key is with all of our estate documents. All our passwords are with our estate documents.

*Thoughts* - This letter will be one of the most important financial documents you can write to your spouse. You can help eliminate many headaches in the aftermath of an unexpected death. The list above is just an example of some of the assets you may hold. Your list should reflect your current assets. Keep a computer file with this letter and make the necessary corrections as your financial picture changes. This letter is not designed to be all-inclusive but only an outline for quick reference. My "In Case I Die Letter" is the first page in my estate book, with more detailed information in their respective files.

If you have frozen your spouse's credit, put that in the list above, as it will cause problems if your spouse needs to borrow money after your death. Also, ensure your spouse has immediate access to any accounts if a need arises to withdraw funds for your funeral arrangements.

If you have unusual items such as airplanes, boats, recreational vehicles, and rare coins and artifacts, you should list an agency or friend for your spouse to contact to sell those items. A representative can help save your spouse some money if your spouse is not familiar with the current value of some unique items in your possession.

You can also store important documents online if you would like. Google Docs will let you store up to 15 GB for free. Digital vault apps like Presidio also cost about $10 monthly and will store all your estate files.

You can also purchase a product like the Nokbox, which stands for next of kin box. It is a fireproof box containing 15 categories to place your important documents into, with a checklist inside each file to inform you what papers to add.

# Chapter 19

## Transfer on Death Deeds

P*urpose* - A Transfer on Death or TOD deed lets a homeowner transfer property to a beneficiary and avoid the probate process.

*Highlights* - A Transfer on Death deed is a great tool and can help in estate planning. It is a low-cost way to avoid probate and may save you money in the long run. A Transfer on Death deed will also give you a step-up in the cost basis of the house, saving you taxes on any property appreciation. A Transfer on Death deed is not allowed in all states.

This type of deed may also be known as a Beneficiary Deed, Deed upon Death, or a Transfer-on-Death Instrument.

As a property owner, if your state allows a transfer of deed upon death, you can follow this five-step process to complete the deed change:

First, you will need to find out the requirements and the specific form or forms for which you will need to change the language on the deed.

Second, you must decide whom you want the property to transfer to upon death. You can choose a person or persons, a charity, or an organization. You must be specific and use full names to list your beneficiaries to ensure the deed is not contested in a court of law. If your state allows Joint Tenants, you can use that language, meaning that if one of your beneficiaries dies before you do, the other beneficiary will become the new owner.

Third, on the Transfer on Death deed form, you must list a legal description of the property. You can take this description off the current deed and transcribe it verbatim.

Fourth, if you and your spouse are the only property owners, then both of you will have to sign the form. Some states will require you to have a witness or witnesses also sign the form. If you need witnesses, wait to sign the form until the witnesses verify it is your signature.

Fifth, you will need to file the deed with the county recorder. You should be able to find the location of your county recorder's office online. Check to see if they require a fee to change the deed. If you mail in the form, you must follow up and ensure that the new form has been added to your original deed and that all the signatures and legal descriptions are valid.

Last, I would give a copy of the new Transfer of Death deed to all the new beneficiaries you listed on the form so they will also have a record.

*Thoughts* - If your state does not allow a TOD deed, other options are available to avoid probate. You can set up a revocable living trust for your property so it will avoid probate. You will have to fund the trust, which will be more expensive than just filling out a transfer of deed form. You can change the trust any time you want since it is revocable. If your state eventually changes the law and establishes a Transfer on Death deed policy, you can cancel the trust and complete the TOD form.

Another option available to you is to change your deed to joint ownership. As a parent or parents, you can add a child or children to the deed with rights of survivorship. Changing the deed will give the new joint owner(s) full interest in the property. Upon the death of the original owner(s), the property will then be transferred to the new beneficiaries to avoid probate. However, the new owners will not get the step-up in cost basis of the property. They will have to pay taxes on any gains from the original sale price of the property. If your state adopts a TOD deed, you can change the joint deed to a Transfer-on-Death deed as described previously.

In 2023, the following 31 states allow transfer-on-death deeds: Alaska, Arizona, Arkansas, California, Colorado, District of Columbia, Hawaii, Illinois, Indiana, Kansas, Maine, Minnesota, Mississippi, Missouri, Montana, Nebraska, Nevada, New Mexico, North Dakota, Ohio, Oklahoma, Oregon, South Dakota, Texas, Utah, Virginia, Washington, West Virginia, Wisconsin, and Wyoming.

*Note - Michigan has a "Lady Bird" deed that functions like a transfer-on-death deed.

# Chapter 20

## Umbrella Insurance

*Purpose* - Umbrella insurance is additional insurance that can add an extra layer of protection for your family.

*Highlights* - Umbrella insurance can help provide additional coverage for lawsuits, property damages, personal injuries, and liability coverage.

A million-dollar umbrella insurance policy may cost upwards of $300 yearly, which is cheaper when compared to other insurance products. Your insurance price will depend on risk factors, including having a dog, how many properties you want to include, and how many vehicles you may own. Also, many umbrella policies will require that you have a minimum liability on your cars and home before they will insure you. As with any insurance policy, your exact price will depend on individual risk factors, including the number of people in your household and how many cars and properties you own.

Many financial advisors recommend you get umbrella insurance if your assets exceed $500,000. They also recommend having the policy coverage equal to your non-protected assets. For example, if you have retirement accounts like 401Ks, IRAs, and irrevocable trusts, those investments will be protected from lawsuits, while some of your other assets may not be covered. If your non-protected assets equal a million dollars, you would want a million-dollar umbrella policy to protect those assets.

You may need an umbrella policy even if you have little in assets. New drivers in your household will carry more risk and may require more insurance to protect your family assets. In addition, an umbrella policy can protect you if you rent property, coach, or participate in sports beyond public or private schooling. Also, if you own a swimming pool or any other risks involving people congregating on your property, an umbrella policy can protect you.

Umbrella policies will not cover any vehicles not listed in the policy. If you purchase a boat, you need to update your umbrella policy, not just the insurance for the boat itself. In addition, umbrella policies will not cover your personal belongings since homeowners and car insurance are designed to protect those items. Generally, umbrella insurance will not cover a home-based business either.

Many insurers who sell umbrella policies will also want you to buy home and auto insurance from them before they sell you an umbrella policy. If you bundle all your insurance products with one company, you may receive up to a 20% discount. Bundling can save you money in the long run and put all your insurance products with one company. However, bundling may be an added risk if that particular insurance company is not financially sound. Still, bundling is the best practice and will give you better pricing. If you decide not to bundle, seek a stand-alone policy from a highly rated company.

In general, it is financially cheaper to purchase an umbrella policy rather than to increase the liability on your home or vehicle.

*Thoughts* - The more assets you have, the higher your chance of being sued. Lawyers will go after the person with the deepest pockets to pay their clients. An umbrella policy will also cover all defense and court costs if your estate is sued.

The relatively inexpensive price of an umbrella policy can bring you peace of mind and let you sleep at night. For the cost, it is the cheapest insurance to protect your assets.

# Chapter 21

Long Term Care Insurance

P *urpose* - Long-term care can provide services and support if you cannot provide care for yourself.

*Highlights* - Long-term care may be divided into two categories: community and residential care or home-based care.

Long-term community care could be an adult senior care living center, which can house many residents. This facility will provide participants with meals, social activities, personal care, and exercise. A residential care facility, much like a nursing or assisted living home, can also offer similar care but on a smaller scale.

There are various levels of care. Some facilities may provide limited care, such as housekeeping and cleaning, whereas others may offer more programs like memory care or other specialized programs.

Home-based long-term care is provided at home by friends and or family members. This care can help with daily activities like cooking, dressing, bathing, and taking medications. Sometimes, home-based care will also use paid employees, who may include therapists, nurses, and other medical professionals.

Many of us will need long-term care at some point in our lives. Predicting when this type of care will be required and to what extent can be challenging. Sometimes, the need for long-term care may arise suddenly after a heart attack or an unexpected injury. For most of us, the need for long-term care may slowly occur over the years as we age.

Long-term care insurance generally comes in three types of policies: traditional, hybrid, or a long-term care rider. Traditional long-term care insurance is a standalone insurance policy and covers only long-term care expenses. It will pay any associated costs for a facility or for care in your home. These types of long-term care policies are becoming more expensive and difficult to obtain. The premiums on traditional long-term care can increase over time and have a "use it or lose it" aspect. In other words, if you do not need long-term care, then you will lose all the premiums you paid into the policy.

A hybrid long-term care insurance policy is linked to a permanent life insurance policy or an annuity. The premium is guaranteed for a lifetime but is usually higher than a traditional long-term care policy since it also offers life insurance. A hybrid policy can accrue a cash value that can be used to pay for long-term care needs. Any cash value you do not use for long-term care needs will pass to your beneficiaries upon your death.

Similar to a hybrid policy, a rider is an addition to a life insurance policy. This addition will most likely increase your premiums above your current level. You will be able to use a certain percentage of your death benefit to pay for any long-term care expenses.

You can also pay long-term care premiums and out-of-pocket costs with an HSA, FSA, or HRA savings plan. You cannot use funds in these accounts to pay life insurance premiums. Suppose your long-term care policy is linked to a life insurance product. In that case, you must ensure the insurance company splits or bifurcates the bill to differentiate the premiums between the two products.

If you elect to purchase a long-term care policy, most insurers will have an elimination period of up to 90 days before paying any bills. After 90 days, the insurance company may still require that you have disabilities where you cannot perform daily functions and need a long-term care facility.

*Thoughts* - Purchasing long-term care insurance can be expensive, but the alternative can be even more costly. Generally, long-term care is not covered by health insurance or Medicare. For this reason, consider purchasing long-term care insurance. Typically, there are a few ways to do this.

If you are younger and have the budget to afford long-term care, talk to your spouse to see if you want to bundle it with an insurance policy. If you are retired and your budget is below your pension, you can take some extra income and purchase long-term care insurance. If you do not want to use those options, I recommend designating some of your investments to help pay for any long-term care needs that may arise in the future.

A healthy lifestyle is the best way to prevent or reduce time in a long-term care facility. Getting plenty of exercise and eating nutritious food can be the best medicine for delaying or eliminating long-term care. The longer we can lead an active lifestyle, the better.

# Chapter 22

## Retirement

P*urpose* - Retirement is when you have enough assets not to work full-time to support yourself or your family.

*Highlights* - One of the most important financial decisions you will make is whether to retire or keep working. If you enjoy your job and you want to continue working, then by all means don't stop. There is no requirement to stop working until the day we die. Some people may be hesitant to change and might not be mentally ready to retire, even if they can financially retire. Sit down and discuss with your spouse and reconfirm the direction you want to go.

If you decide to retire, calculate a "retirement years" budget six months before your estimated retirement. You should expect your expenses to change since you have been operating under a "working years" budget. My transportation and entertainment expenses dropped in retirement. My medical and travel expenses increased, leaving us with almost the same budget as before retirement. Once you know your retirement budget, you can then calculate if your pensions and social security benefits will be enough to support your budget. If you do not have enough income, you will probably have to supplement your income with investment assets. Also, if you plan to convert pre-tax money to post-tax money, you can expect hefty taxes if you do not deduct those taxes from your pre-tax investments.

One investment rule of thumb to see if you have enough to retire is to have saved 12 times your salary. For example, if you have wages of $60,000, you should have at least $720,000 in savings or investments. With this amount of money, you have a reasonable chance not to outlive your assets. As with everything, this rule of thumb can be adjusted depending on sources of income in retirement.

If you are still deciding about retirement, consider working part time. You will still bring in a paycheck and not deplete all your investments by working fewer hours. This approach to working later in life can ease you into retirement if you are not ready. If, after some time, you miss working full time, then switch back to full time. If working part time suits you, then continue until you are ready to retire from the workforce altogether. Many people take on a volunteer job after retiring to keep them busy. By volunteering, you can pass on your wisdom and knowledge or even help charity organizations. Many of these organizations are always in need of volunteers.

During my retirement, I was shocked at how much I missed all my male fellowship at work. I love staying home and going to the gym with my wife, but I immediately saw she needed a break from me. At my old job, I loved talking about flying with all my buddies as we were all pilots. So, in turn, I needed to find an outlet where I could reminisce with all my old flying buddies, which got me into cooking. Once a month, I head out to the local airport to feed the workers. We all sit around and eat while talking about flying. This new fellowship met my need to talk about flying and gave my wife a break from my being around the house all the time.

If you decide to retire, and you have a stay-at-home spouse, remember she still has her full-time job running the entire household. You will need to change your habits and start helping with the various chores around the house. This way, you can take the load from your spouse and let her enjoy part-time work as well. Helping out around the home will pay big dividends, trust me.

*Thoughts* - I have seen some people retire from their current job and take another job with considerably less pay. There is nothing wrong with taking a lower-salary position that you might enjoy more. By staying on budget and contributing to your investments in a higher-paying job, you could take a job you consider more enjoyable in retirement without worrying about income.

Retirement is not for everyone, and you may not be ready. Others will love it and wonder how they ever had time to go to work. I thought I would always play golf, but in reality, I hardly ever get to play golf as I seem so busy with other projects. The biggest thing in retirement is, like the song says, "Be Happy." If you are not happy, then change the situation. Whatever you do, don't look back. Keep moving forward.

The only difference between time and money is that you can make more money, but you cannot make more time. Enjoy retirement to its fullest.

# Chapter 23

## Pensions - Defined Benefit Plans

P*urpose* - A defined benefit pension plan is a retirement program that promises to pay you periodic payments for the rest of your and possibly your spouse's life.

*Highlights* - Federal, state, and private companies may offer defined benefit pension plans. The amount of your pension depends on many factors, including years of service, rank, age, contributions, and being fully vested.

An employer assumes all the investment risk in a defined benefit pension plan. The employer controls the plan's funding and how the funds are invested. The employer also pays all the fees associated with managing the plan.

Your right to a future benefit or payment is called vesting. Vesting in your employer's pension plan can happen immediately or may take as long as seven years. If you leave employment before vesting, you may lose all or part of your pension.

A defined benefit plan may give you a choice of taking a lump sum or periodic payments in the form of an annuity. These regular payments can be monthly or even yearly for the rest of your life, including your spouse, depending on what annuity option you select. Some employers may allow you to take a certain percentage in a lump sum payout and the rest in an annuity payout. The decision to take your pension in a lump sum or an annuity payout depends on several factors. Does your spouse already have a pension? Will you both get Social Security pensions? What is your employer's financial condition? These are all questions to ask before you and your spouse decide what option to select. If your employer is a private sector company offering a defined benefit pension, they must enroll in the Pension Benefit Guaranty Corporation or PBGC program. The PBGC is a government-run insurance program to protect employees if their company defaults. If your company defaults on pensions, the PBGC will step in and pay a portion of your annuity up to the legal limit. This limit may be less than you were receiving from your company.

Some pensions will have annual cost of living adjustments to their plans. Many government and state pensions will match the previous year's inflation rate or slightly below. Most private corporations do not offer annual cost of living adjustments to their pension options.

All governments and private companies' pension plans generally offer a few different options to choose from. Those choices may include a Single Life Only Annuity, Joint Annuity, and a Single Life Monthly Guaranteed Annuity.

The Single Life Only Annuity pays you monthly benefits for your lifetime, but no benefits are available to your spouse or any other beneficiary after your death. The Single Life Only Annuity option usually pays the highest monthly benefit. If you are married and select the Single Life option, you may want to consider purchasing life insurance since the payments will cease upon your death.

The Joint and Survivor Annuity insures both you and your spouse/ dependent. The monthly benefits will be less than the Single Life Annuity, typically around 10%, since this option insures two lives instead of one. Upon your death, the Joint and Survivor Annuity will continue to pay approximately 50% of the reduced benefit until the death of your spouse. For example, if your Single Life Annuity pays $60,000 per year in benefits, then the Joint Survivor Annuity will pay 10% less or around $54,000 per year in benefits to you and your spouse.

Upon your death, the Joint and Survivor Annuity would be reduced by 50% of the $54,000 and pay your spouse $27,000 until his or her death. If your spouse dies before you, then you will still receive the $54,000 benefit until your death. Your employer may offer other types of Joint Survivor Annuities besides the 50%. They may include options like 66%, 75%, or 100% Joint and Survivor Annuities.

Another annuity option your employer may offer is a Single Life Annuity with a monthly guarantee. The monthly guarantee selected can be from 5 to 20 years after starting benefits. This type of annuity will guarantee payment to you or a beneficiary for the time frame chosen, even if you die during that time frame. For example, if you choose a 20-year guaranteed annuity and die after five years of receiving benefits, this option will continue paying your beneficiary for another 15 years and then stop. If after the 20-year period ends and the employee is still alive, this option will continue to pay until the employee dies. A 20-year guarantee option will be reduced by approximately 12% (age dependent) of the Single Life Annuity option. In our example above, the 20-year guarantee option would pay $52,800 for 20 years as a 60-year-old retiree.

When you retire, the payments of your pension may be fully taxable. If your employer funded your plan without any of your contributions, your monthly check would be subject to federal and possibly state taxes. If you contributed after-tax money to your pension plan, your pension will be partially taxable.

*Thoughts* - If you have a defined benefit plan with your company or employer, you have hit the jackpot. Employers, including governments, are eliminating these plans as I write. Many are switching to 401K plans, where the employee takes all the financial risk.

There are many factors to think about when choosing an annuity option. Are you and your spouse healthy? If only you are healthy, you may want a Single Life Annuity with a life insurance policy. If you and your spouse are healthy, then the Joint and Survivor benefit may be your best choice. If you have to care for a dependent child, then the Single Life Annuity with a 20-year guarantee may be the best option. You and your spouse should go through all the choices together. In reality, all the options pay approximately the same amount if you and your spouse live to your life expectancies.

A defined benefit pension plan can provide a guaranteed monthly check for the rest of your life. If you have additional investment in a separate 401K or IRA plan, you have some flexibility with your finances. You may want to purchase an annuity if your employer does not offer a defined benefit pension. We will cover that option in the next chapter.

# Chapter 24

## Annuities

P*urpose* - To provide periodic monthly or annual payments for your lifetime.

*Highlights* - If you have only Social Security to rely on in retirement, you might want to supplement that monthly income by purchasing an annuity. An annuity is an insurance contract sold through investment companies, banks, insurance agents, and financial planners.

Annuities are broken down into two basic categories: deferred annuities and income annuities.

*Deferred Annuity* - A deferred annuity is tax-deferred and has no IRS limits on contributions. The money you contribute to the annuity is paid with after-tax money and will have a cost basis. Any investment gains in the account will grow tax-deferred until you set up the annuity to pay income. Most investors will maximize their 401K and IRA contributions before contributing extra money to an annuity. Generally, annuities will not have Required Minimum Distributions if the contract has periodic payments.

Annuities, like 401Ks and IRAs, are subject to the IRS rules for any withdrawals. If you take a distribution before age 59.5, you may be subject to a 10% IRS penalty. There are a few exceptions where you can take the money early and avoid penalties.

Deferred annuities usually come in two varieties: variable and fixed. Deferred variable annuities from investment companies will let you invest in various mutual funds on their platform. These mutual funds can be the same funds found in your 401K or IRA accounts. Annuities may include additional charges to include annual fees not found in 401K or IRA accounts. These extra annuity expenses have been reduced over the years and have become more competitive. Remember, with a deferred variable annuity invested in mutual funds, you will bear the market risk and could lose money.

A deferred fixed annuity can provide a guaranteed rate of return, much like a Certificate of Deposit. This type of investment is not FDIC or SPIC insured like a Certificate of Deposit, but the risk is minimal. Investment companies will generally offer you a few fixed-income mutual funds to invest in.

*Income Annuities* - An income annuity is where you either annuitize a deferred annuity or take a lump sum of money and buy an immediate annuity. An income annuity will provide you with an income stream of money for your lifetime or over any other period of time. For example, say you want to buy an annuity with a lump sum; you can take some 401K or IRA money and purchase a single or joint life annuity.

If you select a single, joint, or time period income annuity, your payment will not be affected by market fluctuations, thus giving you peace of mind that you will get the same pay each month for as long as you are alive.

Immediate variable income annuities will provide a monthly payment, but the amount is not guaranteed. This type of annuity can offer growth opportunities to help keep up with inflation, but the payments may depend on the investments inside the annuity.

*Thoughts* - Do you need to invest in or buy an annuity? You will have to look at your entire portfolio to answer that question.

If you are investment-rich and pension-poor, you may need to invest in or buy an annuity. What is investment-rich? In the retirement topic, I talk about having a recommended 12 times your salary in investments to be able to retire comfortably. If you have considerably more than this amount, you may want to take some of that money and buy an annuity. For example, say you have two Social Security payments and no other pensions. Your Social Security payments come to $40,000 yearly, and your annual budget is $60,000. In this scenario, you may want to buy an annuity to compensate for the $20,000 budget shortfall. A $20,000 per year single life annuity will cost approximately $261,502 for a 65-year-old male. Adding the annuity to your Social Security payments will match your $60,000 yearly budget. With inflation eating away at your budget each year, you may want to purchase an annuity slightly above your budget to give you a few years of breathing room. By following this method, you can live below your budget for a few years. If or when your income falls below your budget, you may withdraw some money from your investments to make up for the shortfall.

If you are investment-rich and pension-rich, I want to congratulate you on a job well done. In this scenario, you will likely not need to purchase an additional annuity. For example, in the illustration above, you have a military pension and two Social Security payments, giving you $90,000 a year in income. If you have the same budget of $60,000 per year, you are living well below your means and would not need the additional income an annuity would provide.

If you are investment-poor and pension-rich, you will likely not need to purchase an additional annuity. In this scenario, continue to live below your means while letting your investments increase in value to give you a better safety net.

If you are investment-poor and pension-poor, consider working additional years to make sure your Social Security payments can equal your budget. You may need to reduce the cost of your lifestyle to meet your future income.

# Chapter 25

## Dividends and Capital Gains

P*urpose* - To provide additional income for retirement with the possibility of paying less in taxes.

*Highlights* - If you do not want to buy an annuity and have only Social Security income to rely on, you can purchase stocks or mutual funds that pay dividends or capital gains. This type of investment can provide you with a regular stream of income. You can buy dividend stocks or purchase mutual funds that pay dividends and capital gains. Generally, we have dividends and capital gains reinvested back into our investment accounts during our working years. In retirement, you can deposit those dividends and capital gains directly into your bank account.

If you want to purchase dividend stocks, you must realize that buying individual stocks may have more risk than purchasing a dividend mutual fund, which will own many stocks. You can even play dividend stocks off each other if you want. For example, you could buy Verizon and AT&T stock, two large telecom companies in the same industry. Generally, both of these stocks consistently pay significant dividends. As of this writing, Verizon is paying 6.45% dividends per year, and AT&T is paying 4.73% per year. It may seem risky to own dividend stocks from the same industry, but I don't see anyone giving up their cell phones in the near term. Both of these companies are sound and generate large revenues. Both Verizon and AT&T pay dividends quarterly. Understand that these dividends are variable and will change over time. You should not depend on a certain dividend payout to meet your budget.

To be conservative, you should expect a more reasonable dividend percentage of maybe 5%. This lower percentage would give you some breathing room in your budgeting. As in previous examples, if you are short on your budget by $20,000 per year, you would need approximately $200,000 in each of these companies to figure a conservative 5% dividend payout. You could purchase two dividend-paying stocks in different industries to lower your risk.

In addition, you could purchase a mutual fund that pays dividends. A mutual fund would hold many dividend stocks, thus lowering your risk. Also, many mutual funds will pay capital gains when they buy and sell stocks within their fund. In most cases, capital gains will be paid out at the end of the year, while dividends are usually paid quarterly. Remember, whatever percentage of dividends and capital gains are paid out, the stock or mutual fund will decrease by that same percentage in price.

There can also be tax advantages to purchasing mutual funds that pay qualified dividends. You have to hold that stock or mutual fund for more than 60 days in the 121 days that began 60 days before the ex-dividend date for the dividend to be qualified. Qualified dividends for 2025 are taxed at 0%, 15%, or 20%, depending on your taxable income and filing status. Non-qualified dividends, or dividends that do not meet the above requirement, will be taxed at your ordinary tax rate.

You can also get another tax advantage for long-term capital gain distributions. In 2025, the long-term capital gains tax rate will also be 0%, 15%, or 20% for most assets held for over a year. Assets held for less than a year, or short-term capital gains, will be taxed at your ordinary tax rate.

*Thoughts* - If you want to avoid buying an annuity, investing in stocks or mutual funds that pay dividends and capital gains can be an excellent option. This option will let you keep the principal, whereas when buying an annuity, you would have to give up your money in exchange for periodic payments. Buying stocks or mutual funds that pay dividends and capital gains can be more appealing if you die, because your heirs will at least get the principal.

This approach to generating additional income is purely variable, since dividends and capital gains can change over time and may not provide the income you were planning for. However, this is still a great option to generate additional revenue to meet your budget.

# Chapter 26

## Reverse Mortgages and Home Equity Line of Credit

P*urpose* - Reverse mortgages and Home Equity Lines of Credit are loan options for homeowners to borrow money based on the equity in their home.

*Highlights* - If you are cash- or investment-poor but equity-rich in your home, consider a reverse mortgage. Many older people want to stay in their homes for as long as possible, and this type of financial product can make that happen.

You may qualify for a reverse mortgage if you are at least 62 or older. You will need to live in your home and have some equity built up or have your home paid off outright. A reverse mortgage can enable you to borrow money based on the equity you have in your home. You can then use that money for whatever you want while staying in your house.

A reverse mortgage can also have its downsides. Your debt against your house will keep increasing as you owe interest and possibly fees over time. The debt may eventually equal the equity you have in your home. If you need to transition to assisted living or long-term care facilities, you might not have any extra money left over when you sell your home. If this is the case, you may need to budget any money you get from a reverse mortgage to last you for the rest of your life.

With a reverse mortgage, the lender may send you the funds in one lump sum payment, a series of monthly payments, or some combination of the two. The reverse mortgage loan must be paid back when you die or when your estate sells your home.

If you decide to obtain a reverse mortgage, you are still responsible for paying the insurance and taxes on your home. You must also continue to live in your house.

Another alternative when borrowing against the equity in your house is a home equity line of credit called a HELOC loan. With a HELOC, you will have a "draw period" during which you can borrow money. Once the "draw period" ends, you must start paying the loan back plus interest. The time to pay the loan back is called the "repayment period." Unlike a reverse mortgage, if you have a HELOC loan, you can still sell your house, but the sale proceeds must be used to pay off the loan first.

HELOCs can carry some risk. While an original home loan may have a fixed interest rate, HELOCs use variable interest rates that can rise or fall depending on the financial markets. You could lose your home to foreclosure if you cannot repay your HELOC.

*Thoughts* - If you plan on staying in your house for a short time, I would not get a reverse mortgage as it may be too costly. Also, if you are unmarried and living with another person, check the contract to see if they can live in the house after your death. Many live-in partners have experienced a rude awakening upon discovering that the home they were living in now belongs to the reverse mortgage company after their partner's death.

If you decide to get a reverse mortgage, ensure you get a "non-recourse" clause. Almost all reverse mortgages have this clause, but verify it is in your contract. This clause means that your loan cannot be greater than the value of your home and that any debt will not pass to your estate or your heirs when the house is sold.

A reverse mortgage and a HELOC can provide additional income, but both loans are costly. Ensure you know the fees and rules before borrowing money against the equity in your home.

# Chapter 27

## Social Security

P*urpose* - To provide retirement income to individuals, families, and people with disabilities.

*Highlights* - You will need to work for ten years or have 40 work credits to qualify for Social Security. You can earn up to four work credits per year based on your annual earnings. Social Security tax is deducted from your wages as FICA, which stands for Federal Insurance Contributions Act. Your taxation will be 6.2% of your salary, and your employer will also pay a matching tax of 6.2%. In all, 12.4% of your wages will be taxed for Social Security up to the FICA limit.

You may elect to take Social Security between 62 and 70 if not disabled. Your Full Retirement Age (FRA) depends on when you were born. If you were born in 1960 or later, then your FRA is age 67. If you take Social Security earlier than your FRA, your benefit will be reduced accordingly. If you decide to take benefits at age 62, your benefits will be reduced, and you will get only 70% of what your FRA benefit would have been. For example, if your benefits were projected to be $1,000 at age 67 (FRA), your monthly check at age 62 would be $700 or 70% of $1,000. Conversely, your benefits will increase if you delay taking benefits beyond your FRA. By delaying taking benefits until age 70, your monthly check would increase 124% to $1,240 per month. Generally, each year you delay taking Social Security, your benefit will increase by approximately 8%.

You can apply for Social Security benefits at age 61 and nine months. Social Security benefits are paid the following month after you have been eligible for a full month. For example, if you turn 62 on May 3, your first full month of eligibility is June (not May since you were not eligible for the first two days of the month), and your first payment will arrive in July. The one exception to this rule is that if your birthday is on the 1st or 2nd day of the month, you will get your check the following month. Remember, you must be eligible for Social Security for one full month before obtaining a check the next month. You have met the one-month eligibility requirement if you take Social Security benefits any time after your 62nd birth month.

*Spousal Benefits* - You can also collect your Social Security benefit or up to 50% of your spouse's benefit, whichever is higher, at their FRA. The Social Security Administration will automatically pay you the higher benefits. If you take spousal benefits earlier than FRA, those benefits may be reduced to less than 50%. There is no benefit to delaying spousal benefits after your FRA as they do not increase. To qualify as a married spouse, you must be married for at least one continuous year before applying for spousal benefits. You must have been previously married for ten years for a divorced spouse to qualify for spousal benefits. An exception to the ten-year marriage rule is if you care for a child under 16 or a disabled child, you may be eligible for spousal benefits regardless of your age or the number of years married.

*Survivor Benefits* - A surviving spouse who has reached their FRA can receive 100% of the deceased's benefit. If the surviving spouse is between 60 and FRA, they can receive between 71.5% and 99% of that benefit. A disabled spouse aged 50 through 59 can receive 71.5% of that benefit. A surviving spouse caring for a child under age 16 can receive 75% regardless of age. Spouses who are divorced can receive the same percentages if they qualify.

*Working and taking Social Security* - If you are under your FRA for the entire year, Social Security will deduct $1 from your benefit payments for every $2 in earnings above the annual limit. For 2025, that limit is

$23,400. In the year you reach FRA, Social Security will deduct $1 in benefits for every $3 in earnings you earn above $62,160 for 2025.

If you're younger than FRA, and some of your benefits are withheld because your earnings are more than $22,320, there is some good news. About one year after you reach FRA, Social Security will recalculate and increase your benefits to consider those months in which you received no or reduced benefits.

I often get asked if withdrawing money from my 401K counts as wages. The short answer is no. Only your wages count toward Social Security's earnings limits if you work for someone else. For the earnings limits, Social Security counts only your net earnings from self-employment if you're self-employed, not income such as other government benefits, investment earnings, interest, pensions, annuities, and capital gains.

Set up an account on the Social Security website as soon as possible, as they provide lots of information. You can obtain a benefit verification letter; change your address, phone number, and direct deposit; obtain a replacement Medicare card and an SSA -1099 for tax purposes; and view past earnings and future benefits.

If you apply for Social Security before age 65, you will automatically be enrolled in Medicare. A one-time survivor death benefit of $255 will be paid to the surviving spouse or child if there is no living spouse.

*Thoughts* - First, you must ask yourself, do you need Social Security to make your budget, or in case of your death, does your spouse need Social Security to make their budget? If the answer is yes, delay Social Security as long as possible. If the answer is no, then you may want to take your benefits early and invest them. To be able to make this decision, you must know the break-even numbers.

The Social Security website has a break-even chart that illustrates how if one person takes early retirement at age 62 and a second person with the same benefits takes their retirement at their FRA, or age 67 in this example, they will both break even in the amount of benefits they will receive at approximately 78 years of age. So it takes approximately 11 years for a person who took their social security at age 67 to catch up to those who took their benefits at age 62.

If you need Social Security benefits to meet your budget and your life expectancy is projected to be greater than 78, consider delaying benefits as long as possible. Remember, this chart assumes you will need your benefits for your budget.

What if you or your spouse (if you die) do not need Social Security benefits to make your budget? Should you delay taking Social Security, or should you take the benefits and invest them? You can use a simple investment calculator to determine the break-even point if you decide to invest your Social Security benefits. Suppose you take your Social Security benefits at age 62 and invest the benefits at a 4% annual return. Compare that outcome to taking benefits at age 67 and investing the proceeds at a 4% annual return. In that case, the break-even point is 18 years or 85 years of age.

To recap, if you spend your Social Security benefits, the break-even point is age 78. If you invest your Social Security benefits at 4% annually, the break-even point is age 85. If we use the same example above and invest the benefits with a 6% return, the break-even point is 27 years or 94 years of age. If your life expectancy is less than the break-even points in the above examples, you may want to take your benefits early and invest them.

Knowing your life expectancy can help you decide whether you want to take Social Security benefits early or not. The average life expectancy of a 62-year-old male on the Social Security website is 21.5 years or 83.5 years of age. For a female, it is 24.4 years or 86.4 years of age.

*Overall* - I would not take Social Security benefits if you are working. By taking the benefits earlier, you may have your benefits reduced, as mentioned above, or the benefits may move you into a higher tax bracket. If you need Social Security benefits to make your retirement budget, delay as long as possible. If you do not need your Social Security benefits to make your budget, consider taking those benefits early and investing them. Make sure you talk this over with your spouse and a financial planner.

# Chapter 28

## Medicare

P*urpose* - Medicare is a federal health insurance program for people 65 and older or people younger than 65 with certain disabilities.

*Highlights* - You will want to sign up for Medicare three months before turning 65; you will automatically be signed up if you have already started drawing Social Security benefits.

You are eligible for Medicare on the 1st day of the month you turn 65. If your birthday is on the 1st day of the month, you then become eligible for Medicare on the 1st day of the month prior to your 65th birthday.

If you are eligible for Social Security Disability Insurance (SSDI), you are also eligible for Medicare benefits after you meet the 24-month qualifying period. If you cannot work for at least a year, you can apply for SSDI and Medicare insurance. For some disabilities, you may be eligible for Medicare immediately. A few examples include people with End-Stage Renal Disease (permanent kidney failure requiring dialysis or a transplant, sometimes called ESRD), cancers, ALS, and respiratory illnesses.

*Medicare Part A is hospital coverage* and covers inpatient hospital stays, care in a skilled nursing facility, hospice care, and home health care. You will automatically be enrolled in Part A when you apply for Medicare.

Taxes for Medicare Part A are deducted from your wages during your working years. Medicare will deduct 1.45% of your wages, and your employer must match 1.45% for a 2.9% total in taxes.

Medicare also has an additional tax of 0.9% on all wages above \$200,000 (\$250,000 for joint returns, \$125,000 for married taxpayers filing separate returns).

Medicare Part A charges a deductible each time you are admitted to the hospital. It can change every year, but for 2025, the deductible is \$1,676. You can buy supplemental insurance to pay for this deductible and any out-of-pocket costs that Part A will not pay. Supplemental plans such as Medigap or Tricare for Life (for former military) can cover these costs.

Medicare Part A pays for virtually all hospital services for the first 60 days you're in the hospital. Some exceptions exist; for example, Medicare Part A will not pay for a private room.

If you are a U.S. citizen or permanent resident and have not worked long enough to qualify for Medicare, you may be able to buy into the program by paying a Part A premium. The monthly premium for Part A can be as much as \$518 for 2025.

<u>Medicare Part B is medical insurance coverage</u> and covers certain doctors' services, outpatient care, ambulance transportation, medical supplies, and preventive services.

Medicare Part B involves more costs, and you may want to defer signing up for Part B if you are still working and have insurance through your job or are covered by your spouse's health plan. But if you do not have other insurance and don't sign up for Part B when you first enroll in Medicare, you'll likely have to pay a higher monthly premium as a penalty for as long as you're in the program. It is important to note Part A is what you pay for while working, and Part B is what you pay once you enroll in Medicare.

The federal government sets the Part B monthly premiums and deductibles each year. In 2025, the premium is \$185.00 per person, with an annual deductible of $257. Generally, all recipients must pay this premium if they are signed up for Medicare at age 65. This premium will cover 80% of Part B expenses. As mentioned above, you can purchase additional insurance coverage to cover that 20% gap, like Medigap or Tricare for Life.

Also, Medicare Part B is subject to additional Medicare premiums if your income exceeds $106,000 single or $212,000 married in 2025. These additional Medicare premiums are called Income Related Monthly Adjustment Amounts (IRMAA). IRMAA will be discussed in the next Chapter.

*Medicare Part C is Medicare Advantage*, a Medicare-approved plan from a private company that offers an alternative to original Medicare for your health and drug coverage. These "bundled" plans include Part A, Part B, and usually Part D. Plans may offer some extra benefits that original Medicare doesn't cover, such as vision, hearing, and dental services. Medicare Advantage Plans have yearly contracts with Medicare and must follow Medicare's coverage rules. The Medicare Advantage Plan must notify you about any changes before the start of the next enrollment year.

The federal government requires these plans to cover everything that original Medicare covers. In addition, in recent years, the Centers for Medicare and Medicaid Services, which sets the rules for Medicare, has allowed Medicare Advantage Plans to cover such extras as wheelchair ramps and shower grips for your home, meal delivery, and transportation to and from doctors' offices.

Medicare Advantage Plans are generally Health Maintenance Organizations (HMOs) or Preferred Provider Organizations (PPOs). In HMOs, you will typically choose a primary care doctor who will then direct your care and will usually have to refer you to a specialist. PPOs have networks of doctors you can see and facilities you can use, sometimes without a referral. Generally, you will have to stay in the plan network for medical care for Medicare Advantage Plans.

Medicare Advantage can be more affordable for people with long-term health issues.

*Medicare Part D is prescription drug coverage* that helps pay for prescription drugs you may need. To get Medicare drug coverage, you must join a Medicare-approved plan that offers drug coverage. In addition, Medicare Advantage drug plans must also be Medicare approved.

Each plan can vary in costs and the drugs they cover but must give at least a standard level of coverage set by Medicare. Medicare drug coverage includes generic and brand-name medications. Depending on the different tiers, plans can vary the list of prescription drugs they cover. How much you pay for each drug depends on which plan you choose. For 2025, the maximum Part D deductible is $590 annually

Each plan generally has some premiums and out-of-pocket costs. Some will have flat co-pays for each medication or a percentage of the prescription costs in addition to an annual deductible. Starting in 2025 the out-of-pocket cost will be capped at $2,000.

In 2020, the "doughnut hole" was eliminated, and a participant will pay at most 25% of the cost of brand-name and generic prescriptions.

If you do not enroll in Medicare Part D without other insurance at age 65, you will get a late enrollment penalty. The amount is typically 1% of the national base beneficiary premium for each whole, uncovered month that the participant didn't have Part D or other creditable coverage. The national base beneficiary premium for 2025 is $36.78.

In addition, Medicare Part D is also subject to the IRMAA or extra Medicare tax, just like Part B.

*Thoughts -* The most significant decision with Medicare is whether you want to go with the Original Medicare, i.e., Parts A and B, or whether you want to apply also for Medicare Advantage Part C. The other decision is whether you wish to purchase a Medicare supplement to pay for the 20% that Medicare Part B does not pay.

# Chapter 29

Income Related Monthly Adjustment Amount

P*urpose* - People enrolled in Medicare with higher incomes will have to pay extra Medicare Part B and D premiums. Five income brackets operate on a sliding scale with Income Related Monthly Adjustment Amounts (IRMAA).

*Highlights* - Medicare beneficiaries who are single and earn over $106,000 or married and earn over $212,000 in 2025 will have to pay the IRMAA higher premiums.

For Medicare beneficiaries who receive Social Security retirement benefits, the premium for Part B is deducted from their Social Security check. Part B premiums are deducted regardless of whether the person is subject to the IRMAA surcharge. However, the "hold harmless" provision that prevents Social Security checks from decreasing from one year to the next does not apply to people who pay the IRMAA surcharge.

You don't need to opt in or sign up for the IRMAA. If you are required to pay a surcharge, the Social Security Administration will send you a letter alerting you to the higher cost.

IRMAA is calculated from the income you made two years prior to the year the premium is to be paid. Medicare will use your prior year's tax filings to get your income information. For example, in 2025, Medicare will calculate your 2023 income to determine if any IRMAA premiums are due in 2026.

The annual Medicare IRMAA is determined using a person's modified adjusted gross income (MAGI) from two years prior. MAGI is your adjusted gross income (AGI) plus student loan interest, IRA contributions, passive income loss, deductions for tuition and fees, taxable Social Security payments, untaxed foreign income, non-taxable Social Security benefits, and tax-exempt interest. MAGI is identical or very close to your adjusted gross income for many filers. MAGI doesn't include Supplemental Security Income (SSI).

You can appeal the IRMAA determination if you believe your calculations are in error. Suppose you've had a life-changing event, including marriage, divorce, the death of a spouse, loss of income, income reduction, pension loss, or loss of rental property; you can file an appeal using Form SSA-44.

*Thoughts* - IRMAA does not affect everyone in retirement, as a married couple would have to make over $212,000 in 2025 for the extra Medicare premiums to kick in. However, people who are still working past age 63 and have income over this limit may be affected when they turn 65 and enroll in Medicare Part B and Part D.

One issue where IRMAA may affect retirees is when converting pre-tax money to post-tax money, i.e., converting Traditional IRA/401K pre-tax money to Roth IRA/401K post-tax. Pre-tax income will be added to any other income and may increase your income over the $212,000 limit for a married couple in 2025.

Once retired, you should talk to a financial advisor and devise a game plan on when to convert any pre-tax money to post-tax accounts. You are not required to convert this money until the Required Minimum Distributions (RMD) kicks in at age 73, but you may want to start converting this money earlier than age 73. I will talk about Required Minimum Distributions in the next chapter.

IRMAA can bite you, so you need to be aware of its five income tax brackets while working.

# Chapter 30

Required Minimum Distributions

P*urpose* - The age at which you must start taking Required Minimum Distributions (RMDs) from pre-tax employer-sponsored retirement plans and IRAs.

*Highlights* - You have to take RMDs from your 401(k), profit-sharing, 403(b), or other defined contribution plan by April 1 following the later of the calendar year in which you reach age 72 (73 if you reach age 72 after Dec. 31, 2022), or retire (if your plan allows this). The same rules apply to all IRAs, including SEPs and SIMPLE IRAs. For each year after your required beginning date, you must withdraw your RMD by December 31st of that year. If you don't take any distributions, or if the distributions are not large enough, you may have to pay a penalty. Secure Act 2.0 in 2023 reduced the penalty to a 25% excise tax on the amount not distributed as required.

The minimum distribution rules apply to original account holders and their beneficiaries in these types of plans: Traditional IRAs, SEP IRAs, SIMPLE IRAs, 401(k) plans, 403(b) plans, 457(b) plans, profit sharing plans, other defined contribution plans, and Roth IRA beneficiaries. Note that the original account holders of Roth IRAs and Roth 401Ks are not required to take an RMD.

The minimum distribution amount is calculated on your account balance at the end of the previous year using a life expectancy table provided by the IRS. Each year, your calculation will be different since the balance of your account and the IRS life expectancy numbers will change.

*Thoughts* - Although you are legally required to start this conversion process only at the required age of 72 or 73, starting earlier may be more advantageous.

One reason to start converting pre-tax to post-tax is the current tax rates. If tax rates are scheduled to go up, it may be beneficial to begin converting earlier to reduce the taxes you will owe.

Another reason is the unexpected death of a spouse. If this happens, the surviving spouse will now be in the single tax bracket for Federal taxes and the Single tax bracket for IRMAA, i.e., $106,000 for 2025. This unexpected death will probably increase your taxes, whereas if you had started the conversion process earlier with both spouses alive, you might have been in a lower tax bracket. I advise people that after retirement or age 63, consult with a financial planner and come up with a plan for when to convert pre-tax money to post-tax accounts.

I always print out the current year's IRMAA tax bracket and federal tax brackets so I can determine how much money I may want to convert from a Traditional IRA to a Roth IRA. I target a tax bracket that I can live with and then use the following formula. In this example, I will use the 2025 Federal 24% married tax bracket with an annual income of $120,000 (including all pensions and Social Security withdrawals). The formula is the top level of the 24% tax bracket + two standard deductions - Annual Income = Amount available to convert to post-tax and remain in the 24% tax bracket. In this case, the top level of the 24% married tax bracket for 2025 is $394,600 + $30,000 (two standard deductions) = $424,600 - $120,000 (annual income) = $304,600 amount available to convert to a Roth IRA while staying in the 24% married tax bracket.

When converting a large amount of money, you can take the federal and state taxes out of the pre-tax account or pay the taxes quarterly. By paying the taxes quarterly, you ensure a greater amount of post-tax or

Roth investment will stay in the account. However, paying hefty federal and state taxes quarterly can be challenging. Talk with your spouse and financial planner about the best course of action.

# Chapter 31

## Annual Gift and Lifetime Exclusions

P*urpose* - The annual gift exclusion is the maximum amount of money or property you can give another individual per year without filling out any IRS tax forms.

*Highlights* - The annual gift exclusion for 2025 is $19,000 per person per year. If you exceed the annual gift exclusion amount, you must file an IRS Form 709. Any excess will count towards your lifetime gift exclusion amount. If you are married, you and your spouse can each give $19,000 for 2025 to the same individual for a combined total of $38,000 without filing an IRS Form 709.

The lifetime gift exclusion for 2025 is $13.99M per person or $27.98M for married couples. Once you exceed your lifetime exclusion, you may owe taxes on any gifts over the annual gift exclusion. Generally, the giver is the one responsible for paying taxes. You cannot deduct gifts from your taxes if given to family members or friends; only qualified charitable organizations are eligible.

If you exceed your lifetime gift exclusion, the gift tax rates range from 18% to 40%. On January 1, 2026, the lifetime gift exclusion is scheduled to revert to the 2018 levels.

*Thoughts* - Most of us will likely be below the lifetime gift exclusion and will not have to pay any gift taxes. If you go over the annual gift exclusion amount, just fill out the IRS Form 709. The biggest issue is giving property over the annual gift amount and forgetting to fill out the 709 form.

Any gifts given to a spouse who is a U.S. citizen are not counted as a gift for IRS purposes. Also, funds paid to educational and medical facilities on behalf of another person do not count against the annual gift tax amount.

I used the annual gift exclusion to help my niece and nephew get started in investing. My wife and I helped set up their accounts and told the kids we would partner with them in investing. Each quarter, we give them a small amount of money to invest. At first, we helped them select a few good mutual funds, but now they decide what funds they want to invest in. When partnering with new investors, ensure they understand this is not their spending account but their investment account for retirement. When kids or young adults see their balances grow over time, they get excited and will take responsibility for investing in their future.

# Chapter 32

Qualified Charitable Distributions

P*urpose* - A Qualified Charitable Distribution (QCD) lets you withdraw money from an IRA and give it to a qualified charity tax-free.

*Highlights* - To be able to participate in a QCD, you must be age 70.5 or older. You can distribute a limit of $100,000 per year to a qualified charitable organization. A QCD can come from all IRAs: Traditional, Roth, Simple, and SEP. You cannot use a QCD from a 401K plan, so you will have to rollover to an IRA plan. Money used in a QCD qualifies towards your Required Minimum Distributions. You cannot itemize a QCD donation on your taxes. QCD's are tax-free from Federal taxes. State taxes will depend on which state you live in.

*Thoughts* - This is an excellent program for which you must develop a plan before age 70.5. In other words, you may want to convert only some of your pre-tax money into post-tax accounts to take advantage of QCDs.

For example, say you are over 70.5 years old in retirement, and your annual retirement income is $90,000 or $7,500 monthly. You tithe or give away to charity 10% or $750 each month to your local church or charity. Now, you decide to tithe the entire year using the QCD. You would have your financial institution send a QCD check from your IRA for $9,000 ($750 x 12) to your local church without ever paying Federal taxes on that money. In this case, you are tithing for the entire year and do not have to deduct the $750 from your monthly budget.

If you are in the 22% tax bracket for married filing jointly, you just saved $1,980 in Federal taxes for the year.

If you decide you would like to take advantage of the QCD program, calculate your life expectancy from age 70.5, multiply that by your future expected yearly tithe or charity amount, and leave that money in a pre-tax IRA account. For example, if your life expectancy is 84, you would have at least 13 years to participate in the QCD program. Assuming your annual tithing would stay at $9,000 yearly from the example above, times 13 years would give you $117,000. Leave that amount in the pre-tax program, and do not convert it to post-tax or Roth IRA, thus saving $25,740 in federal taxes. Typically, you would expect the $117,000 to grow over those 13 years, enabling a spouse to continue participating in the QCD program if he or she outlives you.

Since the QCD rules are not allowed for a 401K plan, you can rollover the $117,000 amount from your Traditional 401K plan into a pre-tax or Traditional IRA without paying any taxes and then start your QCDs from the IRA account. You can move funds from the 401K plan to the IRA plan if you are retired and above age 55 or actively employed and above age 59.5 and not get hit with an IRS penalty.

I had never heard of QCDs until a few years ago. A friend of mine was conversing with a financial planner, who explained the basics of the charitable program to him. A few days later, in a conversation with my friend, he explained QCDs to me. This process of relaying financial strategies back and forth among friends changed our financial plans for the future.

# Chapter 33

## Hospice

P*urpose* - Hospice focuses on the care, comfort, and quality of life of a person with a serious illness approaching the end of life.

*Highlights* - Patients are eligible for hospice care when diagnosed with a terminal illness with a prognosis of six months or less to live. Only a doctor can make this prognosis. At that time, comfort care, and symptom management become the primary focus, and curative treatment is no longer the patient's choice or option.

Discussing hospice options should happen any time the patient has been diagnosed with a life-limiting illness.

Hospice care is provided in a setting that best meets the needs of each patient and family. The most common setting is the patient's home. Hospice care is also provided in nursing homes, assisted living facilities, and hospitals, whichever suits the patient's needs.

Hospice care brings together a team of people with special skills, like nurses, doctors, social workers, spiritual advisors, and trained volunteers. Everyone works with the patient, the caregiver, and the family to provide the medical, emotional, and spiritual support needed.

You qualify for hospice care if you have Medicare Part A and meet all of these conditions: Your Hospice doctor and your regular doctor certify that you're terminally ill with a life expectancy of six months or less; you accept comfort care or palliative care instead of care to cure your illness; you sign a statement choosing hospice care instead of other Medicare-covered treatments for your terminal illness and related conditions.

You pay nothing for hospice care. You pay a co-payment of up to $5 for each prescription for outpatient drugs for pain and symptom management. If the hospice benefit doesn't cover your medication, your hospice provider should contact your plan to see if Medicare Part D covers it. You may have to pay 5% of the Medicare-Approved Amount for inpatient respite care, i.e., someone else temporarily looking after you. Your copay can't exceed the inpatient hospital deductible for the year. Original Medicare will still pay for covered benefits for health problems not part of your terminal illness and related conditions, but this is unusual.

Once you choose hospice care, your hospice benefit will usually cover everything you need. Medicare doesn't cover room and board if you get hospice care in your home or if you live in a nursing home or a hospice inpatient facility.

Medicaid may also pay for Hospice care in most states. Medicaid is a joint federal and state program. People become eligible for Medicaid when their income and assets are at a certain level. Medicaid will provide nearly identical benefits to Medicare.

The Veterans Health Administration will also cover Hospice care. If you are a veteran, check to see if you are eligible. These benefits are very similar to Medicare hospice benefits.

Hospice does not provide 24-hour in-home care but does provide intermittent nursing visits to assess, monitor, and treat symptoms, as well as teach family and caregivers the skills they need to care for the patient.

You may want to obtain a healthcare proxy for a family member in hospice. A health care proxy is a representative who can make health care decisions if you cannot communicate this yourself and who will work closely with your health care team to ensure your care and treatment preferences are followed.

*Thoughts* - Hospice is about living. Hospice strives to bring quality of life and comfort to each patient and the family. Often, patients will feel better with good pain and symptom management. Hospice is an experience of care and support, different from any other type of care.

Bereavement Services follow family and caregivers for a year following the patient's death. These services may include personal visits, providing information concerning the grieving process, and offering periodic opportunities for group support. Bereavement Services provides information and referrals to other area resources when needed.

# Chapter 34

Burial and Last Wishes

*Purpose* - To ensure you get the funeral and burial you desire.

*Highlights* - The Federal Trade Commission (FTC) controls the regulations for what funeral providers can charge. In 1984, the FTC established the Funeral Rule to give consumers of funeral services certain protections. The rule's main objective was to ensure consumers receive adequate information concerning all goods and services they may purchase from a funeral provider.

Funeral pricing generally falls into three categories: essential or basic services, charges for other services and merchandise, and cash advances. The provider must provide a detailed list of all the costs. The regulations allow customers to pick and choose exactly what they want.

Funeral providers are allowed to charge a basic service fee that customers must pay. The basic services fee includes services common to all funerals, regardless of the specific arrangement. These include funeral planning, securing the necessary permits and copies of death certificates, preparing the notices, sheltering the remains, and coordinating the arrangements with the cemetery, crematory, or other third parties.

Charges for other services and merchandise include costs for optional goods and services such as transporting the remains; embalming and other preparation; use of the funeral home for the viewing, ceremony, or memorial service; use of equipment and staff for a graveside service; use of a hearse or limousine; a casket, outer burial container or alternate container; and cremation or interment.

Cash advances are fees charged by the funeral home for goods and services it buys from outside vendors on your behalf, including flowers, obituary notices, pallbearers, officiating clergy, and organists and soloists. Some funeral providers charge you their cost for the items they buy on your behalf. Others may add a service fee to this cost.

Many funeral homes require embalming if you're planning a viewing or visitation. Generally, embalming is not necessary or legally required if the body is buried or cremated shortly after death. Eliminating this service can save you hundreds of dollars.

A casket is often the most expensive item you'll buy if you plan a traditional full-service funeral. Caskets vary widely in style and price and are sold primarily for visual appeal. Typically, caskets are constructed of metal, wood, fiberboard, fiberglass, or plastic. The cost for a casket can range from $2,000 to $10,000.

Many families who choose to have their loved ones cremated rent a casket from the funeral home for the visitation and funeral, eliminating the cost of buying a casket. For those who choose a direct cremation without a viewing or other ceremony where the body is present, the funeral provider must offer an inexpensive unfinished wood box or alternative container, a non-metal enclosure, cardboard, or canvas, that is cremated with the body. The funeral home can then provide the ashes to you for any last wishes.

Military veterans and their dependents may also receive burial benefits for their time in the military. Benefits may include a gravesite in any of the VA national cemeteries with available space; opening and closing of the grave; perpetual care; a government headstone, marker, or medallion; a burial flag; and a Presidential Memorial Certificate, at no cost to the family. Burial benefits are also available for spouses and dependents buried in a national cemetery, including burial with the veteran, perpetual care, and the spouse or dependents' name and date of birth and death inscribed on the Veteran's headstone at no cost to the family. Eligible spouses and dependents may be buried, even if they predecease the veteran.

*Thoughts* - It may be challenging to pre-plan or pre-pay for burial services in today's environment. Our country is much more mobile than it was decades ago, and many older parents may relocate to an area where their children reside.

If you have made it through all the other financial decisions in life, and it is in your power, then why not tackle your end-of-life financial decision? It will give you peace of mind that you will get what you desire and save indecision or squabbling from your children if they have disagreements on what might have been your last wishes.

My wife's grandparents, Thelma and DJ, pre-planned and pre-paid for their deaths. They picked out the caskets, headstones, burial sites, and even the meals served to guests. Their family members did not have to take care of any details, which, in turn, made the funerals easier for all parties.

# Conclusion

I wanted to highlight a few things I have learned over three decades in finance. You will make mistakes. I made many mistakes. That is inevitable. Warren Buffet makes mistakes, too. With diversification you can limit the damage. When I first started investing, I paid little attention to the word diversification, but as I got older, I realized how vital diversification is in finance. If you are well-diversified, you can sleep soundly at night. If you do not sleep well at night, that is a red flag, and you and your spouse need to make some changes.

It is essential always to look at your investments in the long term and where you want to be financially at that future time. Minor budget cuts can add up over time. Do you need that $60 streaming bill each month? That $60 is $720 per year or $7,200 over ten years. What if I invested that money in a mutual fund that averages 8% yearly return? That $60 bill now becomes over $11,000 in 10 years or over $195,000 in 40 years. That is the time value of investing. After 40 years, that $60 bill will cost you $28,800, but redirecting that bill and investing it with an 8% return will get you $195,000. I encourage you to look at that $60 bill differently now. Little budget cuts early on can have a significant impact on your retirement years down the road. So when you review all your financial decisions, don't just look at the cost in today's dollars, but look at it over time.

Doing an end-of-year review of all your financial accounts is essential. Do you need to change beneficiaries? Did you have another child? Do you need to update your life insurance or obtain more umbrella insurance? Each year, you should thoroughly review all your financial decisions with your spouse to see if both are where you want to be and if you are achieving your goals.

Do not get discouraged by financial setbacks. They are going to happen whether you like it or not. There will be times when you need help finding investments that you are comfortable with. You could adopt a buy-and-hold strategy, let it ride, and not worry about the markets. A buy-and-hold strategy can be harder to do than many people think. What if you have $100,000 in the market and lose $20,000? Will you be okay with that? What if you have $1,000,000 in the market and lose $200,000? The bigger the numbers, the more difficult the loss seems, even though it is the same percentage.

Plan accordingly about five years before your target date for retirement. You do not have to go wholly conservative but start asking yourself some questions. Can I still retire if I lose 20% or 30% of my investments? If the answer is no, you might consider moving to a more conservative investment. Retiring when the markets are going up is always better than retiring in a down market. The unknown of how low the financial market will go can weigh on a person if starting retirement. If you have a pension and can live below your means, this can give you some stability to retire even during a down market.

My dad was a commodity broker, and I always asked him which way he thought the market was heading. He responded that it may go up or down, and he has never been wrong. There is some wisdom in that statement, as you don't have any meaningful control over the market yourself. Remember, the stock market has come back 100% of the time, as my dad always reminded me.

Every investment product has its time. Do not love or hate a particular investment, stock, or mutual fund. People who may have lost money in a particular investment or stock swear they will never invest in that again. Every investment will have its days that shine and its days that it will decline, so do not disregard any investment because you may have lost money or had a bad experience.

Last, I want to caution you on "a hot investment tip." These tips are a dime a dozen in the finance field. Be careful. Do not make any financial decisions on a whim; always talk to your spouse before making investment decisions. My wife has often kept me from making poor financial decisions in our marriage. Always keep your spouse in the financial loop. That is the single best financial advice I can ever give you.

# About the Author

Don Pickinpaugh obtained an MBA in Financial Risk Management. He spent 13 years at a major airline helping to manage two multi-billion dollar Defined Contribution retirement plans. He has written hundreds of articles on various financial topics.

www.ingramcontent.com/pod-product-compliance
Lightning Source LLC
LaVergne TN
LVHW022059200926
848481LV00003B/987